WITHDRAWN

ONE MAN'S WAR IN KOREA

By the same author

One Man's SAS

One Man's War in Korea

LOFTY LARGE

WILLIAM KIMBER

First published in 1988

British Library Cataloguing in Publication Data

Large, Lofty
One man's war in Korea
1. Korean War. — Biographies
I. Title
951.9′042′0924

ISBN 0-7183-0696-1

*William Kimber & Co Ltd is part of the
Thorsons Publishing Group,
Wellingborough, Northamptonshire,
NN8 2RQ, England.*

Photoset in North Wales by
Derek Doyle & Associates Mold, Clwyd.
Printed in Great Britain by
Redwood Burn Limited, Trowbridge, Wiltshire

1 3 5 7 9 10 8 6 4 2

To those who survived the war in Korea

In memory of those who didn't

Ours – with cool calculation, sheer terror, screaming agony, savage anger and timely compassion – not to reason why?

Contents

TROG

In the Oxford English Dictionary –
TROGLODYTE *– Cave Dweller*

In the British Army –
TROG – Abbreviation of Troglodyte
> *Term applied only to Non-Commissioned Ranks of any Army or real military force. Soldiers, like cave dwellers, must sometimes live in holes in the ground to survive.*

Forewarning

Most non-fictional military books are written by historians or officers. Historians deal usually with grand strategies and how they were implemented by Generals in the field. Officers rarely mention any form of life militarily lower than the lowest commissioned rank, so that when 'Rupert did his splendid attack' the reader is often left with the impression that 'Rupert' was a 'one man war' and if he happened to be a platoon commander it is likely those unmentionable, funny little 'trogs', his platoon, were watching the 'splendid attack' in awe, from a place of safety. Much as all those good old craftsmen watched in amazement as Christopher Wren built St Paul's Cathedral.

So, having waited thirty-odd years after my first military action, hoping someone with a better story and more able to write it would do so, it has eventually sunk in. If you want something done – do it yourself! What I have written, except where stated, is what I have seen, heard or done myself. This is only the story of one man, a typical infantry trog. Not an exceptional trog, just an ordinary Brit whose experience was twisted this way and that by the unpredictable hand of Fate.

There are (have been and will be) many men in the British Armed Forces who would have made a much better job of my situations than did I. Lady Luck, who rarely – if ever – lets me win anything is usually gracious enough to smile upon me when the shit hits the fan. So I have survived where better men have perished.

Experience gained in what might be regarded by most people as 'adverse conditions' has made me very proud to have been a trog, British and part of the British Army. Any trog, in any army in the world who is not proud of his unit, his army, his country, may have my sympathies, but he is not worth his salt.

The men of the Gloucestershire Regiment, with whom I gained my first operational experience were, of course, mostly good old West Country men with a high percentage from Gloucestershire. But there were men from all parts of the British Isles in the regiment, it was a good cross section of the British population and a better unit would be hard to find – anywhere in the world. History and the friends I had in all the other units of 29 Independent Infantry Brigade in Korea lead me to the belief that the Glosters were in good company.

As all men are different it is possible (perhaps probable) that, in battle, my sensations, feelings, etc; were not typical of other men involved. Some of the things written by me may offend some people but, although my profession was the sword, not the pen, that which is written is an honest attempt to describe the situations of one man.

This book and its other half (already published as *One Man's SAS*) were originally written so that when the 'brats' ask, 'What did you do in the Army, Dad?' I could maybe open one eye and say, 'Read the bloody book'.

The system is called 'Planning for Peace'. Another cock-up, it's brought nothing but aggro so far.

CHAPTER ONE

Devizes

Joining the British Army was a very natural step to take – even at the tender age of fifteen.

Natural that is, because I had always wanted to be a soldier, as far back as I could remember, and my father, a farmworker, always promised faithfully that if I ever worked on a farm he'd split my stupid skull with his big axe. After leaving school at the age of fourteen, my parents first lined me up for a career in the food industry by getting me a job as a baker's boy. Didn't last long though, about three or four months I think. Then to forestry, pulling out timber with horses mostly, on the steep western slopes of the Cotswold hills, above Winchcombe, where tractors could not operate. Hard work, more of a man's job and more rewarding. Many of my workmates were Austrian POWs. This was 1945 and the war in Europe was drawing to a close. I felt sorry for some of the prisoners; although they were obviously well treated, they thought constantly of their families back home.

Little did I think then …

Probably it was at Christmas 1945, when an uncle came visiting and when he realised I was just kicking my heels waiting to be old enough for the Army he said he was sure I could enlist as a 'drummerboy or something'. He promised to find out when he returned home, to somewhere near Aldershot.He kept his promise and on 15 February 1946 I arrived at Devizes, depot of the Wiltshire Regiment, to begin a new life.

Had I mentioned earlier that I lived in North Gloucestershire, you'd probably say 'Why the hell the Wiltshire Regiment?' Now that I have mentioned it – a good question.

Being only fifteen years old and dead set on being a real soldier I had to be an infantryman or nothing. The only way to join the infantry in those days, at that age was to join as a band-boy. There were no vacancies in the Glosters' band at that time so I opted for the nearest on offer.

The Army Recruiting staff at Cheltenham had tried very hard to talk me into being a guardsman as, even then, I was over six foot tall. Also, I found out later, the Recruiter would have been paid five shillings (25p) if I joined the guards but only half of that if I joined anything else!

Having just lived some very formative years through World War Two, even an ignorant country bumpkin knew damn well that bullshit and ancient uniforms had nothing to do with winning. To spend my time stamping and standing around looking useless to be gazed at by all and sundry had no appeal whatsoever. Anyway, to Devizes, a small market town almost swamped by the military. Thousands of troops, Poles, Dutch and probably other nationalities. A POW camp for German prisoners and Le Marchant Barracks, Depot, The Wiltshire Regiment.

For the next two years I wasted my time (as I thought) trying to grow up, waiting and wanting to be old enough to somehow get out of the band and get to grips with the real Army. Those two years at Devizes worked out fairly well in retrospect, as I laid the foundations to escape from military music, learned self discipline and made a lot of good friends.

A band-boy's life was a hard one by today's standards. The rules were plentiful and strictly enforced. The first rules I heard took some beating: 'You will not smoke, you will not drink, you will not associate with women.' Like waving a rag at a bull. We were not allowed out of camp during the week, had to be in bed by 9 p.m. every night. (Saturday and Sunday included.) Once a month – if we were lucky – we were allowed a 36-hour pass – 1p.m. Saturday to 8.30p.m. Sunday. Every evening during the week we had supervised individual practice with our band instruments, from 6p.m. to 7p.m.

There were about 25 to 30 boys with the band at that time. All our spare time was spent scrubbing, polishing, bullshit and breaking every damn rule we could lay our hands on.

On Sunday mornings we had to parade in our World War *One* uniforms, survive a thorough inspection, march to church in the town, and back. A few weeks after joining the Army, I was smoking, drinking and have been an agnostic ever since.

There was a slight brake on social life. Our pay was not too hot, ten bob (50p) per week. We were not allowed to draw ten bob though, only five bob (25p). And that didn't happen either.

Sweets were on ration, and every week we would get our ration when we were paid (without choice). Then of course there was that old Army racket, 'Barrack Damages'. Every week the paying officer would drop two half crowns on the table in front of me, I would then move to the next table to change one half crown for a florin (10p) and my sweet ration, – usually a Mars Bar and a small bar of Cadbury's Plain. Then to the next table to change my other half crown for another florin and watch them tick off my name as having paid 'barrack damages'. Finally, loaded down with my 20p pay I would rush off to hit the high life.

As a comparision of pay, a Regular Army private was on about £2 to £3 per week, and a conscript was on 28 bob (£1.40) at that time. Before joining the Army I had been earning five or six pounds per week on the timber job. The Armed Forces were reckoned to be the lowest paid organisation in the country. There was another snag to getting out of barracks. He was called Seedy, (his initials were C.D.) and he was the provost sergeant. His great moment of every week was at 1p.m. on Saturdays, when he could minutely inspect everyone who booked out of barracks and send them back to polish, brush or press something at the slightest whim. I don't remember ever getting sent back, but I used to sweat blood every time Seedy walked around me.

He couldn't read or write but overcame this by various ploys.If he happened to be caught on his own when someone wanted to book out he'd ask their name, pencil in hand, then when they answered he'd scream, 'Well, write it in the book then, you lazy bastard!'

Seedy's prime trick was getting depot orders read to him. He'd pin the orders on the notice board every evening while the boys were at dinner. Then he'd ambush the first one to come past and yell 'Have you read orders yet, Sonny?' Of course the boy would have to say 'no' because, as Seedy well knew, there was no way he could have. There would follow a quick dressing down for being idle, Seedy would then make the unfortunate read the orders loudly from top to bottom. The man who really struck terror into all the band-boys was Bandmaster Dalrymple. His terrible temper was legendary. Anyone unlucky enough to incur his wrath just had no idea what would happen. A kick, a punch or anything which came to hand was likely to land, without warning. I have seen 'Dally' throw a music stand at someone who played a 'Bum note' and destroy half the woodwind section in the process.

Nevertheless, 'Dally' had a heart of gold and always stood firmly between his band and any other authority which sought to interfere. The depot commander always left punishment of band personnel to the bandmaster, he knew the punishment would be far more severe than that normally meted out from the depot office.

I remember some of us spent five evenings scrubbing the band practice room. Dally came in during one session, and watched for a few minutes. To my horror he called my name and when I stood up he said, 'Do you know why you are scrubbing the floor, sonny?' 'Yes, Sir, for breaking out of camp.' 'No, sonny, that was Monday night. The other four nights are for getting bloody well caught!'

Our barrack rooms were small for those days, ten or twelve beds to each room. Bare boards which had to be scrubbed white, an Army cot and a narrow steel wardrobe each. Down the centre of the room, in perfect line and specific formation, were placed the furniture and cleaning utensils. A rifle rack, a six foot folding table, a metal coal tub, (highly polished) a metal bucket, also glittering, one soft sweeping brush, one hard yard brush, a long handled dry floor scrubber and two scrubbing brushes. All the wooden bits had to be scrubbed or scraped whiter than white.

No chairs, no floor coverings or bedside mats, no curtains at the windows. A small open fireplace at the end of the room supplied all the heating and there was no hot water in the washroom. Four weak light bulbs hung from the ceiling. Any dust anywhere was a punishable offence. Dust on a lampshade could be punished by extra inspections for the whole room, or loss of time off at weekends for the person responsible - or for the whole room.

Dirty hands, fingernails, etc. were punished by scrubbing the guilty person. This involved a bath of cold water, lashings of vim and the big yard brush. Two of the biggest boys were always detailed to do the scrubbing (I was always one). If we refused we were scrubbed for condoning filth. I never refused, nor did anyone else. The scrubbing stopped only when we raised blood. I kept myself very clean in those days.

On a weekend off in 1946 I got myself a really good kicking, which eventually put me in hospital for a couple of operations. Having spent about five or six weeks in the Military Hospital at Shaftesbury, I was sent to the Royal Victoria Hospital at Netley, near Southampton, which was then a convalescent depot. When I had almost completed my five weeks' schedule of convalescent training I slipped in my rush for dinner one day, went over a bannister and down a stair-well twenty feet to argue with a concrete floor. The floor won and back I went into a hospital bed for three weeks with a 'badly bruised knee'. At that stage I was offered a medical discharge from the Army. Don't know why, but I refused anyway.

Somewhere during all this hospitalisation, I heard one doctor say to another that it was possible my original injuries would give me trouble when blowing a wind instrument. This gave me a great idea and, when I returned to the band (about March 1947) I took the first opportunity to pass on this gem to the bandmaster, saying of course that a specialist had told me. To my 'great sorrow' I suffered some pain when blowing commenced and was forced to give up band practice.

There then followed a sort of void when no-one knew what to do with me. Knowing that if I didn't look out for myself, I might be out of the frying pan into the fire, I volunteered for Cookhouse fatigues. This may sound madness to all those professional skivers who spent most of their service career dodging such things, but hard work never bothered me and Army rations being what they were I could think of no greater friend to cultivate than the Cook Sergeant.

I must admit, a bit of recce was done before I stuck out my neck for the Cookhouse job. I did not go blindly to the slaughter – rather gladly to the life of Riley.

Along about this time General Montgomery managed to get his way somewhere 'up there' and we were issued with sheets, pillows, pillow cases and – wait for it – pyjamas. There were promises of bedside mats, bedside lockers and other goodies in the pipeline but we left Devizes before any of these appeared.

In any case, a lot of us were suspicious that more kit around would just lead to more bullshit, more kit to be prepared for inspection every Saturday morning and less real spare time.

Kit inspections were the horror of every week. Our kit had to be laid on our beds in a specific order, down to the last tiny item, and squared off to look like it was made of concrete.

Our towels, socks, shirts etc. were stuffed with plywood or stiff cardboard to make them conform. Our spare boots, with thirteen studs in each, and even the soles highly polished had to be in the appropriate place, one upright and one upside down to show the sole. The slightest thing out of place or not quite as it should be and the owner probably saw his bed, with all his kit, thrown out of the barrack window, and had the prospect of another inspection on Sunday morning, irrespective of week-end passes, etc.

On the other side of the coin, I enjoyed the weekly sports afternoon, usually football sometimes boxing, occasionally a cross-country run. Luckily for me, the Army insisted that every boy had two hours' educational training in the afternoon on Monday, Tuesday, Thursday and Friday. This was run by Sergeants of the Royal Army Education Corps, whose patience, dedication, and sheer ability to make anything interesting gave me most of my 'schooling' for life.

CHAPTER TWO

BAOR

In the last few weeks of 1947 the band was expecting to join the battalion, in Germany. In the event we didn't make the move until January 1948. When I joined the band, at Devizes, it was the Band of 2nd Battalion, The Wiltshire Regiment, but in the postwar diminishing of the Army and the granting of Independence to India, the 1st Battalion was brought back from India and amalgamated with the 2nd Battalion in BAOR. The bands amalgamated too, so we became the Band of the 1st Battalion, The Wiltshire Regiment.

Soon after our arrival in Hannover, where the battalion was stationed, six boys were transferred to the battalion's Corps of Drums. I was one of them, and my escape from music was almost complete. I knew that the Corps of Drums was a totally different kettle of fish from the band, and was part of the 'real Army'. I also knew that once I was old enough I could apply for transfer to other units of the Army when volunteers were required. The Paras were top of my list.

Hannover, like almost every other city in Germany, was a shambles of ruins from the war and I realised only too well what the German people must have gone through. In March 1948 I reached the magic age of seventeen and a half and became a man in the eyes of the Army, qualifying for a massive pay rise – from 50p to about £3.00 per week – and more to the point, a cigarette ration!

The fag ration was a hundred and ten per week, which came one hundred one week and one hundred and twenty the next. Cigarettes were the currency of the day. I don't remember all the prices, etc. but a Volkswagen Beetle was said to be one thousand cigarettes. On the seamier side, a 'short time' was two cigarettes and 'all night' was four.

Within a few months of our arrival in Hannover the unit was moved to Krefeld, west of the Rhine, and a better barracks. Before we moved I managed to get poisoned somehow, and had the whole hospital scene again for a week. A stomach pump job saved an early demise but I was as weak as a kitten for days. They told me it was something in the meat I had eaten, so I suppose the odds were stacked against me as I probably ate four times as much as anyone else.

After we reached Krefeld I clicked onto a good skive – from the music scene. Being an ex-boy I had to stay under the control of the bandmaster until I was eighteen years old, at least that's how I remember it, although it doesn't make sense.

The Band was attached to HQ Company for administration purposes, the Corps of Drums was attached to 'B' Company. If I wasn't with the band they assumed I was with the Drums or HQ Company, or 'B' Company, and if I wasn't with anyone they assumed … In that few months I was a loner. The other boys who had transferred with me to the Drums were a bit younger, still had to go to 'school', and do certain parades and things with the band-boys.

I showed up in enough of the right places to keep everyone happy, but managed to join in with all the training I really wanted. Weapon training classes, field training classes, map reading, grenade throwing, a route march, bayonet training, a day on the ranges etc. All done with various platoons of the battalion to which I didn't belong. No one bothered me. After all, who turns up for for training if he doesn't have to?

In the Corps of Drums I became a tenor drummer and 'reserve' bass drummer. The tenor drum is mostly for show – a lot of gyrating drumsticks but very little drumming. The bass drum, on the other hand, controls the beat of the march being played and therefore the marching pace of the troops on parade. If, like me, the bass drummer has long arms he can also indulge in a lot of flashy drumstick work, but it is very tiring.

Few people realise, when they see or hear a military Band and Drums on parade, that there are many things going on within the ranks of musicians which are not very military. It always amazed and amused me when we counter-marched back through our own ranks, giving it all we'd got in the drum and bugle department with a real 'heavy' like 'Sambre et Meuse' we'd hear the familiar rip of 'Twelve Street Rag' coming from the '3rd Clarinets' in the two back ranks of the band.

Twirling drumsticks can be twirled into all sorts of places, and can play havoc with unsuspecting bandsmen. On one big parade, passing through a dense crowd packing the pavements, I saw a pair of familiar and irresistible targets. The drumsticks spun, twirled and did their thing. Too late I realised her boyfriend, a bugler, was right behind me. He nearly blew my head off with that damn bugle, all the way back to barracks.

The Corps of Drums was involved in some good field training. On battalion exercises we were often used as 'enemy'. This could very often get quite hairy. One time in particular, on Sennelager Training Area some of the battalion picked up live ammunition, which was often lying around, and instead of firing blanks they made life quite interesting. I don't think they were really trying to hit us, but they could have fooled me.

Our favourite target when we picked up live 'ammo' in that area, was the weathercock on a big observation tower. Hit it right and it would spin. In fact, I think it was in the shape of a leaping deer rather than the usual weathercock.

The unit was involved in some vast Army exercises during 1949. Exercise 'Agility' was one, and it involved NATO forces of several countries. The thing I remember best of the big exercises was the digging in and moving – it seemed forever. The thousands of infantry moving across open country in great lines and waves. The tanks at night especially. We had a few bad experiences with tanks at night. On one occasion we were on a patrol, and I don't remember what the reason was, but about six of us were scattered along a big overgrown hedge, mostly brambles and thorns, when two lines of tanks (which were harmlessly passing by about two hundred yards away) decided to change direction and came straight through the hedge. One tank passed within a few yards of me as I struggled to get free of the tangle, and when I got clear and realised they were gone through I thought they must have hit someone. When the noise faded away and we had a head-count we found no one was even injured – only scratched.

Although in those days there seemed to be masses of infantry everywhere on field exercises, there were not the quantity of vehicles which dominate field exercises now. Apart from the relatively few trucks which were used to supply the men on foot, and the odd signals or command vehicles around battalion headquarters, there seemed very little transport about, just tanks and armoured cars moving around. When those metal monsters were moving at night it was usually very difficult for us to pinpoint their position or their direction of movement once they left the roads.

The screech and clank of the tanks seemed at times to come from all around us. We would often be lying in the open, in the blackness of night – on at least one occasion in pouring rain – with that screech and clatter everywhere and the ground shaking under us. How the tank crews found their way anywhere at night I have no idea. Of one thing I am sure though; there was no way they could see us.

We heard many stories of people being killed on field exercises at night, but how many were true we didn't know. Most of us took it all with a 'pinch of salt'.

Nevertheless, on those occasions when tank noise filled the night and we lay shivering in the open, the stories we disbelieved in warm daylight became only too possible. Never having had to fight against tanks I can only wonder about it but I always felt that, as an infantryman, it would be easier to fight them (given the right weapons) than to lie on the ground helpless, waiting to be run over.

We got up to some stupid tricks to relieve the boredom, when bullshit reigned supreme. One day, some of us got in an argument about who was a good shot and who wasn't, and somehow it turned out there was a lot of cash laid on the line about shooting a cigarette out of a man's mouth. Two of us were pretty hot under the collar about it all and somehow I found myself standing with my back to a strong wind, with a lighted cigarette between my lips and the other half of the argument sighting a .22 rifle at it from a barrack window 25 yards to my left. He took ages to fire – and missed. Then it was my turn and he refused, saying, 'Not bloody likely, you can't hold still in a wind like that!' The thing that bothered me most was I thought he could hit the damn cigarette easily or I'd never have done it.

Another time, we were practising with mortars in a field firing area, where the grass and brush kept catching fire. We were only using smoke bombs so a couple of us volunteered to stay at the target end and put out the fires while the rest carried on firing. All went well until they forgot about us (so they said) and all four mortars commenced rapid fire. By the time they ran out of bombs it was getting a bit hairy out there.

The interesting thing about the mortar bomb fires is that the same two volunteers were to volunteer again for something stupid – The Korean War.

Bullshit, drill and all that rubbish left me cold. They have always been my great hate. The things that officers organise when they haven't the brains to organise proper training and want to appear in command of the situation. A soldier should not have time to play guardsman if he's to be good at his job. Discipline comes from respect, comradeship and sheer hard training together, not the barrack square, little circles on toe caps, and shiny things.

I realised very young that a smart right turn would not dismiss a mortar shell any more than gleaming brasses deflect a sniper's eye. But the emphasis placed upon these things in some quarters could be misleading. For my first five years in the Army I was almost drowned in bullshit. I am no stranger to little circles on toe-caps, chin straps and even soles of boots. White Blanco on belts, straps, gauntlets, anklets, slings, drum ropes, leathers and almost anything else which would hold still long enough. Cheese-cutters (with or without slashed peak) Leopard skins and all the razzmatazz which was supposed to have frightened the Zulus or someone many years ago, and patently didn't.

I have marched out smartly as right marker for a battalion of infantry which was simmering in bullshit, without raising as much as a snarl from the RSM. So, I have seen my share.

How much better could I have done my job when it really counted if I had been taught to prime a grenade faster, how to keep one eye shut at night and why and when, how to swim faster and further and a whole multitude of things which I had to find out the hard way and sometimes too late. After five years in the infantry I couldn't even read a map properly.

But, there was hope; I was an almost permanent volunteer for transfer. I can't remember all my transfer applications, but it was a very uphill battle. One which nearly came off was stopped when I went into BMH Wuppertal with double pneumonia. Another was stopped in its final days by a broken ankle.

The final failure was my own fault. I wuz conned!! It was early 1950 and the Paras had again asked for volunteers, so I did the usual scribbling and standing on 'orders', red faced, being called a traitor to my Regiment and all that crap. But the transfer application was accepted, went through the channels and all seemed well.

Then one day I was sent for by the company commander, who seemed unusually friendly and said he realised I really meant to get to the Paras eventually, so he had a suggestion to help me. The battalion was moving to Malaya later that year, and we were returning to the UK to re-equip, etc. in the next two or three weeks, so the company commander suggested I transfer as planned, when we got back to the UK, thereby getting a bit of leave and doing my Para training in the UK instead of Germany. Having returned to UK I was ordered to sign a warning order for overseas service before going on leave. On checking with the company office I was assured this would not affect my transfer, so I signed and went on leave. The story was different when I returned from leave.

I had signed the warning order and therefore my transfer to the Paras was cancelled.

It was 17 April 1950 when 1st Battalion The Wiltshire Regiment left its comfortable, centrally heated ex-SS Panzer barracks in Krefeld, Germany, and returned to the Regimental Depot at Devizes, with its long condemned, austere and ancient red brick barracks.

The battalion travelled as such, on the well trammelled route through the Hook of Holland to Harwich, then by troop train to Devizes, where it marched through the town, led by the band and Drums and out on the Swindon Road, north to the barracks. I always claimed I won the race in the front rank of the Drums, to be first man in the gate behind the Drum Major.

One funny story stands out from all those forgotten happenings in Germany: it concerns two hardened old soldiers. One was company commander of HQ Company, a major whose initials were D.I.M. (giving him the obvious nickname). The other was a hard man called Baker, who had been posted to the unit when the wartime SAS was disbanded. Both had done some boxing in their time. Baker was 'on the mat' in front of Dim for some slight misdemeanour and, after hearing the facts of the case, Dim said, 'Well Baker, what will you take – three days confined to barracks, or three rounds in the ring with me?'

Like a flash Baker replied, 'Three rounds in the ring with you, sir!'

Dim considered this shortly, then pronounced sentence:

'Right, seven days to barracks – for taking advantage of an old man!'

Dim was totally unpredictable. One of my friends was made to sit on top of a tall cabinet in Dim's office and sing the National Anthem, in order to get permission to draw a few pounds from his credit balance.

While on field training, Dim had occasion to re-call his jeep, which he had just sent off. Two rounds from his revolver, one of which smashed the windscreen, did the trick.

CHAPTER THREE

To Hong Kong

The only thing of note, which happened in Devizes during those few months of 1950 between arrival from Germany and departure for the Far East, was meeting my future wife. I didn't know it then, of course, but then, who does?

Ann was a nanny, looking after officers' children in the barracks. We both had a good sense of humour and spent many happy hours at week-ends, mostly at her home near Tetbury, and sometimes at my home.

The great snag to our happiness was, of course, the inevitability of the unit's move to warmer climes. When the time came, there was a sad parting at Devizes railway station, promises of 'writing often', and I gave her my 'lucky mascot', a Cornish Jack O'Lantern given to me by a good friend from Cornwall. She still has it. Little did we realise what 'writing often' was going to mean in our lives over the next two and a half years.

The battalion sailed from Southampton on 31 July 1950, bound for Singapore, aboard the troopship *Empire Trooper*. That trip put me off ships for life. The *Empire Trooper* was reputedly the worst boat on the Far East run. I sincerely hope it was.

For those of us in the Corps of Drums, the misery of a 'slow boat to China' was compounded by an absolute gem of man-management that I pray only an officer of the Wiltshire Regiment could think up. In the first day or two out, somewhere in North Biscay, there was organized an inter-platoon competition. Everything from drill, and blind-folded stripping and assembling of Bren guns, to bursting balloons, (thrown overboard) with Brens and rifles. The winning platoon was to be excused training for the rest of the trip, so competition was fierce.

The Corps of Drums won the competition and was duly excused all training for the rest of the trip, which lasted six weeks. Instead we were put on wash-up fatigue, which involved washing up all the food trays for probably about 2,000 men after every meal. We had the privilege of going to the front of the queue at mealtimes so we could get started on time. It took nearly two hours to clean up after each meal, and during that two hours we were in what we called 'the sweat box'. A room thick with steam, hot as hell and twice as nasty. While we spent five or six hours per day in the sweat box, the rest of the battalion spent about two hours per day on training and PT on the open deck, the rest of the day was their own.

It was August when we went through the Red Sea. The pitch sealing the deck planks melted in the heat – in spite of deck shades – and one of the ship's engineer officers died, presumably of heat stroke, also a lad of about twelve who was with the families on board. They were both buried at sea. The heat in the 'sweat box' became unbearable and had us staggering up on deck every ten minutes for a few seconds' gulping of fresh air, thus prolonging our sentence and sealing my resolve to get out from under the clowns running that unit before their brains had to cope with serious military operations.

The Suez Canal was memorable for the 'Bum Boats' at Port Said; selling masses of everything, they flocked around the great troopship, plying their trade. Some of those salesmen must have been among the greatest in the world. One would think that all salesmen would benefit by doing a month's sales course at Port Said. How these men could make a living selling from a small open rowing boat to the ruffians of the British Army 50 feet above them, well the mind boggles at what they might achieve in a smart suit in a car sales room, face to face.

They would first attract the attention of the customer, then bargain for a few minutes, after which a weighted line would be thrown up accurately to the customer who presumably having paid, would then pull up his purchase.

The Suez Canal was also memorable for its 'flashers'. Every so often we would pass by a few camels or donkeys being led by one or two scruffy individuals, and almost always one of these scruffs would lift his 'frock' and flail all he'd got at the passing ship, where he could undoubtedly see the women on the upper decks. I often thought of these Arab flashers when, years later, I was in another Arab country where we were requested not to wear shorts or even roll up our sleeves in case we offended the population.

After the Canal the ancient troopship grumbled slowly south on the Red Sea to call at Aden. Then on into the Indian Ocean, next stop Singapore.

Somewhere in the middle of the Indian Ocean the Korean War began to affect the plans of mice and men. The Argyll and Sutherland Highlanders and the Middlesex Regiment were sent from Hong Kong to Korea, and to fill some of the gap left in Hong Kong we were ordered there instead of Malaya. At the time, some of us wondered how the trogs of the Argylls and the Middlesex battalions would fare, with their sudden move from what was well known in the Army as a 'bullshit posting' to what looked like a real shooting war in Korea.

There were jokes about frightening off the North Koreans with some 'splendid drill parades', or completely blinding them with bullshit. Little did we realise how close to the truth our jokes ran. The British Infantry units from Hong Kong arrived in Korea really well trained to mount guard at Buckingham Palace or baffle the so-called brains of the Army with astounding bullshit. But of the training required 'for a soldier to do what a soldier is for' they had nary a clue. On top of that they had no decent equipment for Korea and practically no usable transport.

Months later word came down the 'trogs grapevine' that the first British units to arrive in Korea had only survived through the incompetence of the enemy, the generosity of the American units with which they came into contact and a lot of thieving at all levels. No doubt this was another unheeded salutary warning to the 'powers that be' that excesses of drill and bullshit could cost very dear in men's lives. The trogs of those two battalions, who formed the basis of 27 (Commonwealth) Brigade deserve a medal each for getting their act together without proper training. They trained the hard way – with the real thing!

Given a fair chance they were as good as anyone and proved it several times over the next few months, but they were literally thrown from the absolute brainless stupidities of those things which plague the real value of 'garrison troops' into the reality of war in about eighteen days. From Hong Kong to the front line in Korea.

Little wonder then, that the first shots fired in Korea by the Middlesex Regiment were (by accident) at each other.

Also thanks, perhaps, to drill and bullshit, no one hit anyone either!!

But that must be another man's story: the Wiltshire Regiment, in the meantime, had been given a new destination.

There followed a great re-organising of 'baggage'and kit on the troopship, so that troops still disembarking at Singapore could get their baggage off before ours. To me, the news of our change of destination was both good and bad. Bad because we were not going to an operational area, which meant another bullshit posting, and instead of the expected four or five weeks on the troopship, we were now sentenced to six weeks for sure. Good, because I had no great urge to get into a shooting war under existing management.

Although the Wiltshire Regiment had a good number of well experienced soldiers in its ranks, among them the Drum Major, an ex-Para who, I believe, had been at Arnhem – there existed a strong feeling of 'us and them' between some officers and the other ranks. Some of us referred to this situation as the 'Ash Plant mentality'. This went back to rehearsals for one of the many bullshit parades in Germany, when there first appeared on Battalion Orders, under the heading Dress for Commissioned Ranks, 'Ash Plants will be carried'. To the ignorant troggery, this conjured images of the clowns coming on parade with little trees, and there were cartoons to be seen depicting some at 'the slope' and some at 'the order' (and others in less military poses).

In the event, 'ash plants' turned out to be walking sticks. I never did find out if we were just out of date, not in touch with the correct military terminology, ignorant of an old regimental custom, or just ignorant.

Morale in the unit had, I think, been adversely affected by too much bullshit. There were so many stupidities that 'yer average trog' couldn't help but doubt the ability of the 'Ruperts'. Morale always tends to go up and down a bit, and it very obviously swung up for training and down for bull.

Eventually, after what seemed like months of the 'sweat box', we got off that damned ship, and found ourselves at Tam-mi Camp about two miles from Yuan Long, in Hong Kong's New Territories. As predicted, bullshit prevailed, but thanks to the genius of the Drum Major we managed to get some decent training, and physical fitness was well catered for. The Corps of

Drums had always had a good share of sportsmen and, backed by a few good triers, they could have a go at anything and be in with a chance.

While attached to 'B' Company we had formed the biggest part of the company, as it had run down strength due to 'demob' of most of its men. 'B' Company were the battalion boxing and seven-a-side football champs when there were only about 30 men in the company – including the roughly 25 men of the Corps of Drums.

In Germany we were lucky enough to have in the company the late Ken Barrington, who afterwards played cricket for his county and England. Ken played cricket for the battalion, but he also shone on the football field, and was a damn good boxer. Somewhere along the way, between Germany and Hong Kong, the Corps of Drums had been shifted from 'B' Company to HQ Company, and HQ being the biggest company (by a couple of hundred) we were not so involved with inter-company sport. One thing we were good at was running up and down the big hills which almost surrounded the camp.

One Saturday night the Drum Major had a drink in the mess and made some rash bets about being able to beat the best times for getting around three or four peaks overlooking the camp. I think there was more than a few quid riding on the outcome. We obviously won – judging by the Drum Major's reactions at the finish, but it came as a shock – while enjoying our Sunday morning 'lie in' – to suddenly find he'd 'volunteered' the lot of us to crack the record before lunch. To be fair though, the Drum Major came with us – hangover and all.

Sometime during the 'rainy season' of late 1950 or early 1951 the battalion had to qualify for pay in the usual manner. Various forced marches, physical tests and fire a range course with rifle, sub-machine gun and light machine-gun.

The physical things went OK as expected, then we moved to Kai-Tak ranges for the weapon classification. We were living in 'pup' tents and 'six man' tents on the ranges. The rain poured down steadily for the whole week we were there. We were shooting for our pay, and at the time I was a three-star soldier, if I qualified in the shooting I would be five-star soon after – probably in March – because of my service time. This would give me a small pay rise.

It was bad enough with the rifle in pouring rain but with the

LMG at five hundred yards I couldn't see the target at all because of the steam coming off the barrel. The commanding officer of the battalion cited Army orders and decreed we would 'classify in the conditions under which we served'. When the results were published, only the CO's batman/driver had qualified out of the whole battalion, and he had never even fired on the ranges. Whether or not this situation was put right by a re-classification under normal conditions I never found out, as I left the unit soon after. Nevertheless if it had not been for a certain Captain Farrar-Hockley I would have lost over £100 in pay over the next two years.

If it's true, as widely believed, that Hitler, Napoleon or someone years ago claimed the British Army were 'lions led by donkeys' the braying in Hong Kong that year must have been heard clear to the Great Wall.

It was in Hong Kong that I first came across that good old Army institution, the 'Char Wallah', one of the greatest concepts the British Army ever brought out of India. Every unit of the Army in India had its Char Wallah. Literally translated Char Wallah means 'tea man', but the Char Wallah was much more than that. I have heard that all Char Wallahs come from the same part of India, but that is just as likely 'trog lore'. I think they are actually from Pakistan, since the sub continent has been divided.

It is possible they originated as water carriers for the Army in India, as immortalised in Rudyard Kipling's poem 'Gunga Din', but, with natural business sense and a lot of hard work under very trying conditions they graduated to canteen, shop, laundry and anything else required by a unit in isolated places. Eventually becoming so organised they travelled around with their units all over the Far East, and were always in demand whether or not the unit was in an isolated place.

They were very 'pro British Army' and took a great pride in 'their' unit. Nowhere was too dangerous for them to go if the unit would allow them. They took a lot of stick from their customers sometimes, but a good unit looked after its Char Wallah, made sure his bills were met and defended him from problems within the unit as well as from without.

I have often thought there is many a British mother, who has probably never heard of Char Wallahs, who owes a great debt of gratitude to some turbanned gentleman of that profession, whose presence in a wild place has helped her young son when he needed it – not perhaps as dramatically as in Kipling's poem, but help nevertheless.

Army rations being what they were, I had a lot of my food from the Char Wallah. His shop was almost always open, day or night, for cups of tea or coffee, soft drinks and a multitude of sandwiches (always called 'Banjos'), always made to order, never stale.

An egg banjo would contain one or two fried eggs depending on the size of egg. A banana banjo would contain one or two bananas (sliced down the middle). Bacon banjo usually contained two huge rashers of good lean bacon.

If we were out in the hills away from camp on normal training, it was likely the Char Wallah would turn up at some time around mid-day with a great urn of tea and a good selection of banjos. He could always find us and be relied upon to have the right food and drink with him.

The Char Wallah's food and drink was always good value for money. At Tam-mi Camp I think there were about five or six Indian 'helpers' who took the Char Wallah's goods around on bicycles. He also employed two oldish Chinese ladies who were brilliant at sewing, mending and darning socks.

When we first arrived at Tam-mi the Char Wallah came around with his 'char and banjos' and, as we bought them, he took our name for his book and gave us a number. After that we just quoted our number when we wanted anything, he would book it down and we would settle the bill every week, usually on pay day.

Another feature of a trog's life in Hong Kong was looking in the newspaper for reports of incoming mail from the UK. The mail was rapidly turning over from sea mail to air mail at that time. There was quite a difference in the price, although I don't remember what it was. Sea mail took at least a month from UK to Hong Kong, whereas air mail took about five or six days, occasionally less.

Ann kept her word and 'wrote often' – about five letters per week, always sending one or two letters by sea mail every week or two, so that when mail arrived by sea I would get some. Air mail arrived in Hong Kong about twice per week at that time, I believe. I don't remember for sure how the newspapers worked it but they gave the date and approximate time of arrival of all

Royal Mail ships and aircraft either the day before they arrived
or on the day of arrival. It was the first thing we looked for in
the daily papers.

I managed to get a good fright on one of our days off. A few
of us went swimming in Castlepeak Bay which was a truck ride
from Tam-mi. Two or three of us swam out to a small rock
about 50 metres from the beach. Climbing onto the rock we
were badly scratched and cut by coral or something, which was
no real problem, and we were having a good laugh at our
misfortune when someone spotted a shark fin a little further
out to sea. Then all those stories of sharks smelling and
'homing in' on blood in the water became only too real. We
probably broke all records for the 50-metre dash getting back
to the beach. That was one of the worst 'terror swims' I've ever
done, but none of us saw any more of the shark.

The famous Spitfire of World War II was still in service with
the RAF and there was at least one squadron of them based in
Hong Kong. I think they were for use in a ground attack role,
and many times when travelling in the back of Army vehicles
we had a Spitfire almost driving down the road behind us.
Then it would lift at what seemed to be the last moment and
pass a few feet above us with a snarling roar of power.
Sometimes, when we were walking in the hills, a Spitfire would
seem to sneak up to us silently – then roar over our heads,
making us duck or dive to the ground. That most beautiful of
all aeroplanes was very common then, but I have rarely seen
one since.

Two amusing incidents stand out in the memories of Hong
Kong. Three or four of us were going for a stroll in the hills
and we stopped to chat to a Chinese farmer who we often saw
when passing that way. I had noticed a square of flat, baked
mud surrounded by concrete about normal kerb height, and
wondered what it was for. It was about four feet square. As I
spoke to the farmer I saw a look of horror on his face and
turned in time to see one of my friends, who had obviously
stood in the little square, crack through the hard crust and
drop almost to his waist in a very sloppy substance which can
only be described by its chemical formula – S.H. ONE.T. In this
case the human kind, specially ripened for use in the paddy
fields. Have you ever forced a cork into an overfull bottle? Yes,
that's what happened, he was covered – nearly to his neck.

Above left 1st Battalion the Wiltshire Regiment reaches the gate of Le Marchant Barracks, Devizes, on its return from Germany, April 1950. The author, front rank drummer, far left (*Wiltshire Gazette*).

Above right A typical wardrobe layout of the 1950s. Photographs such as this were displayed on unit notice boards so there was no excuse for anyone who did not conform — down to the last finest detail! This was for daily room inspection — on Saturdays the kit was usually laid on the soldier's bed, but made to look much smarter and more 'squared off' to exact measurements (*J. Seeney, Sunset Militaria*).

Below Corps of Drums, 1st Wiltshires. Group photo taken in New Territories, Hong Kong, 1951 (*Author's scrapbook*).

Japan, March 1951, just prior to leaving for Korea. Vic on the right, author on the left of the photo. These are the same uniforms we were captured in (*Author's scrapbook*).

At a rest stop for the Glosters' train, somewhere north of Pusan, November 1950 (*S. Mercer*).

Vickers machine-gun position at work in Korea (*The Gloucestershire Regiment Museum*).

A patrol moving through typical Korean countryside (*Imperial War Museum*).

A 4.2-inch Mortar Detachment of 61 Light Regiment, RA. If their support fire was half as good as that given by 'C' Troop, 170 Independent Mortar Battery, RA, when supporting 1st Glosters, then it was brilliant. The whole troop (38 men) was captured or killed in the Imjin battle (*Royal Artillery Institution, Woolwich*).

Some of 2 Platoon, 'A' Company, 1st Glosters, shortly before the Imjin battle. 'A' Company held one of the first positions to feel the full weight of the Chinese offensive and withstood extremely heavy attacks through the night of 22 April (*Roy Mills*).

There followed a mad dash to the nearby river by one mucky mate, while the rest of us, including the farmer, collapsed. (After getting up-wind of course!)

Another time we were in Kowloon railway station, waiting to get the train up to Yuan Long, when a two seat rickshaw pulled up at the entrance with three happy but heavy soldiers in it. They had obviously come a long way and the rickshaw 'boy', who was well built but getting on a bit, was blowing hard. One of his passengers said, 'How much do we owe you, Johnny?' The rickshaw boy replied, 'Oh, you give me what you like.'

The three bright sparks lined up, took off their berets and gave him three cheers, then started towards the station entrance. The rickshaw boy stared in amazement during the three cheers, then collapsed on his shafts with laughter when he realised what was going on. The three saw his sense of humour and came back to pay up. He probably got ten times the normal fare, but could hardly stop laughing to collect it.

So much for 'Oriental inscrutability'. I found the Chinese to have a good sense of humour, and no one can deny their capacity for hard work. Later in life I would find other things to be admired in the Chinese character.

One 'old sweat', who had recently joined us from the Devonshire Regiment, and was a good friend of mine, had a habit of joining Mah-jong parties anywhere he could find them. When we were at Kai Tak ranges he went off into the shanty town nearby and made friends with several Chinese Mah-jong players, coming back a couple of times a bit the worse for local booze.

One night he didn't make it, and says the last thing he remembers is thinking, 'How nice and comfortable they make the ditches around here.' He knew he had just got clear of the shanty town, on the track to the ranges. Two Chinese carried him to the guard room at the range entrance, and in an area well known for 'muggings' etc. he hadn't lost a cent from his rather large roll of dollars.

The same 'old sweat' always pulled the same gimmick on our trips by truck down to Kowloon or Hong Kong. As we passed the San Miguel Brewery he would yell at us all to 'stand up and show respect!' Then he would stand smartly to attention, facing the brewery, and solemnly salute.

Early in 1951 volunteers were required for 1st Glosters in

Korea; my name was first on the list in HQ Company. The Drum Major advised me against going to Korea, but backed me up when he saw I was determined to go. All the NCOs in the Corps of Drums were due to return to the UK within about six months, as their overseas time was up and they were all due for a home posting. I was on the short list for Drum Major, but promotion was no use in a job I didn't want. How could you be a real soldier if you never saw action? Remember, I was always surrounded by men who had seen a lot of action in World War II. In their presence I felt a rookie.

Almost every man jack in the Wiltshire Regiment volunteered for Korea, my chances seemed slim, but somehow I found myself among the 90-odd men allowed to go. There followed six days leave in Hong Kong, then another troopship, His Majesty's Troopship *Empire Orwell* to Kure, Japan. A better ship, and this time no 'sweat box'.

At last I had escaped from everything to do with music in the Army and was heading for a whole new ball game.

My only regret was leaving behind a lot of good friends. Even now, in spite of all that happened, I can honestly say that at no time did I regret leaving the Wiltshire Regiment.

CHAPTER FOUR

Japan – Korea

The trip from Hong Kong to Japan took about five or six days, at the end of which we found ourselves in JRHU (Japan Re-inforcement and Holding Unit) on the outskirts of Kure. The camp at Kure was pretty basic but comfortable by 1951 standards. As it was a Commonwealth Forces Base, run by an Australian contingent, we were on Australian rations. The best rations I can ever remember having. Even I didn't need double rations!

We were re-badged, re-equipped and brought up to scale for the colder climate of Korea, with heavy duty pullovers, extra socks, heavy boots and a newer type of field equipment (1944 pattern).

There followed more medical and dental examinations, carried out en masse in the barrack rooms, twenty odd of us standing by our beds, 'starkers'. More anti this and anti that injections then, after a few days we were sorted out into two groups. One group of about 30, who were troops with battle experience, were sent off to Korea. The rest of us were marched out along country roads for 20-odd miles to the battle camp at Hara-Mura.

I don't remember how long we were at Hara-Mura, two or three weeks I think, and it was well spent. We worked from dawn to dusk – often from dusk to dawn as well – marched miles, and fired all sorts of weapons. We attacked and defended everything in sight the right way and the wrong way to bring out the problems; became accustomed to the crack of bullets passing quite close. The battle school was run by a little, 'oldish' major in the Somerset Light Infantry. He had under his command some of the best and most experienced instructors I have ever seen. They did an excellent job for which I have been forever thankful. There was absolutely no bullshit. We were expected to appear clean and tidy every time we turned out, night or day, rain or shine. Our huts were never given an inspection which we had time to prepare for. (There was little to do to the actual huts except sweep them out as required.) Staff would wander in at any time and expect to find everything clean and tidy.

Weapon cleaning was at an absolute premium, weapons were inspected at any time of the day or night without warning – anywhere we happened to be. We learnt to clean our weapons as soon as possible after firing or carrying in the field. As we never moved around in trucks, always marched, we learnt to clean weapons on the march and during quick five minute breaks at the roadside.

I wish I could remember that major's name. He was white-haired, about five foot three inches tall, had three or four rows of campaign ribbons and was the first real officer I ever met. I have had occasion to be thankful to him many times since. Several times on exercises around Hara-Mura we stopped by farms or isolated houses and were often invited in for a drink of tea, or to have our water bottles replenished. We found the Japanese country folk to be very clean, hardworking and hospitable.

On one occasion I nearly came unstuck when an old farmer gave me a broad wink and poured a clear liquid into my empty water bottle. It looked like water but I was suspicious because he winked, and poured like it was gold. It turned out to be very strong 'Saki', Japanese rice wine. The way it tasted, the half-full water bottle was enough to sink an Army. Anyway, we shared it around and the day felt very much better, much to the delight of the farmer and his family. Had I not noticed, and tipped it down my throat like water they would have had more to laugh about, no doubt.

At the end of the battle course we did a forced march back to JRHU Kure. There we were split into two groups of 30. The second group would leave for Korea about two weeks after the first group. I was with the first group – which, within a few days started on the journey to join our new battalion.

A troop train took us north from Kure to Sasebo, a port on Japan's northern coast. On the way we passed through Hiroshima, where the scars from the atomic bomb of nearly six years before were still visible, but rapidly being built over by man, and grown over by nature. The staging camp at Sasebo was an all American set-up; there were a lot of new things to see and get accustomed to, as we knew we could be involved with American forces in Korea.

Somewhere at Sasebo, perhaps at the entrance to the mess hall there was a great archway over the door, and with bold letters a foot high the statement 'Through these portals pass the world's finest fighting men'. We had never seen anything like it, and the comments drawn were many and varied. Such as, 'How did you know we were coming?' etc.

There is supposedly an old Yorkshire saying, 'What's bummed-up needs bumming up!' – and that about summed up our feelings towards a lot of things we were to encounter from Sasebo onward.

I don't remember staying over-night at Sasebo, I think we went almost straight to the docks and the troopship, - after a meal or two. Somewhere along the way we were called forward and checked off by American staff, probably just before boarding the ship, and a typing error really threw a lot of people into consternation. My Army number is not really an Army number but a regimental number of the Wiltshire Regiment. Instead of the usual eight digits, mine has only seven, so it's different to start with. Don't know how it happened, it must have been a typing error – instead of calling my number, rank and name which was 5577627 Private D. Large, the big American military police sergeant yells out – after a long pause – SS.77627 Private D. Karger. As it came in the right place and I was expecting it, I recognised my last five numbers and answered readily enough. All stared hard as I walked forward and through a doorway. There was a lot of muttering in the background and later I noticed staff pointing me out to others who presumably had not been present at the roll call. Whether or not any of the British Contingent were asked what they were doing with an SS man in the ranks I never heard. No-one asked me anything, in spite of a lot of curious stares. Perhaps being over six feet tall had something to do with that though.

The ship we boarded was an old Japanese troopship. We boarded at night, slept our way over to Pusan, Korea, and were off the ship in the morning. All I remember of the ship was the decks which were covered by thick straw matting on which we slept, and it was small for a troopship. We landed in Korea on 2O March 1951 – being greeted at the quayside and played off

the ship by an all negro American military band whose
marching rendition of 'Saint Louis Blues' was brilliantly
memorable. I wondered if it was a permanent job, and how
many times a day did they have to perform?

Korea, Land of the Morning Calm, was not enjoying many
calm mornings in the early 1950s. In 1945, after World War II,
Korea was divided roughly in half along the 38th Parallel.
North Korea was administered by the Russians so became a
communist State. South Korea, administered by the Americans,
stayed free. There were attempts by the United Nations to hold
free elections throughout Korea so that the country could be
brought together again under one government. Nothing could
be agreed so Korea remained divided. The Russian and
American troops were withdrawn in 1948. On 25 June 1950 the
North Korean Army crossed the 38th Parallel in a
blitzkrieg-type invasion of South Korea.

American forces were deployed to help South Korea in July
1950, other United Nations troops arrived soon after.
Nevertheless, the UN forces were pushed back until, early in
August, they almost had their backs to the sea in what was
called the Pusan Box. In September 1950 a UN offensive
began, which practically destroyed the North Korean Army
and put UN forces almost to the Yalu River, border between
Korea and China.

At that point Communist China entered the war and, catching
UN forces at full stretch from their supply bases, threw in a
massive offensive on 27 November 1950 which sent the UN
reeling back far south beyond the 38th Parallel. By March
1951, UN forces had regained some ground and pushed the
communists back to the general area of the 38th Parallel. The
Land of the Morning Calm had seen some extremely bloody
fighting in that nine months before I first set eyes upon it, and
had been headline news almost constantly. In Pusan we again
came under Commonwealth control, stayed one or two nights,
then boarded a very rough and ready (maybe) troop train for
somewhere a long way north. We were given American rations
to cook and eat on the train.

On the train we were mixed with American troops, some
were new replacements like ourselves, some were men
returning to their units from leave in Japan. The countryside
we passed through had been ravaged by war. By early 1951 a

lot of Korea had seen the front line three or four times, and it showed. Nevertheless people were tilling the fields. Occasionally some paused in their labours to wave at the passing train.

Towns and villages were in ruins, but when we slowed to a crawl – which was often in a built up area – the people looked cheerful, considering their circumstances. Sometimes the train stopped for a few minutes and we would be quickly surrounded by a crowd of mostly children, holding out their hands for the sweets and chocolates which showered from the carriage windows.

American rations seemed to us to contain more sweets and chocolate than real food, so the Korean children did very well for 'goodies' when the Brits came through. At a small station somewhere well up the track the usual crowd of kids were being driven away from the train by American Military Police. This caused a lot of comment from the train, but one single act almost caused more than comment.

There was a woman near the train, with a baby slung on her back in a blanket, the normal method of carrying small children in that part of the world. As the Military Police came along, she started to move away, but not quickly enough for one big sergeant who ran after her, repeatedly lashing her across the shoulders and back with a riding crop, the baby obviously catching a lot of the blows.

There was uproar on the train as Brits and Americans alike yelled their disapproval. A good friend of mine, Vic, leapt to his feet, slammed his bayonet onto his rifle and dived headlong out of the window. He didn't quite make it, I grabbed his belt and hung on. His rifle sling had caught on a metal fitting on the window frame and that held until help arrived, then it took three of us to keep Vic under control for the next few minutes until the train pulled out. Vic was a big lad, normally very quiet and well behaved, but right then he had only one thought, which he let everyone know. 'Let me stick this bastard up his arse and see how he likes it!' Among the uproar on the train I could hear yells indicating that Vic was not on his own trying to leap forth into battle.

As far as I know no one managed to get off, but I hate to think of the consequences if just one or two had broken loose. One American sat near me had pulled his .45 pistol and aimed it at the Military Police before being disarmed. But I didn't know this until afterwards when one of his friends returned it to him – with a lecture. His main excuse was, 'What the hell are we fighting for if that bastard is allowed to live?'

He had a point!

We saw civilian trains sometimes, the ones going south were crowded, with people hanging on the outside of the carriages, and sitting on the roofs. At the side of the track every so often there were the bodies of civilians, men, women and children who had presumably fallen from the crowded trains. Eventually, somewhere, we left the train and were organized onto trucks, with all our kit, to take us to the first of a chain of echelons leading to the battalion, at the front.

The first place we stopped was I think, brigade rear echelon of 29 Independent Infantry Brigade of which 1st Glosters were a part. A night or two there, then on the trucks and a long bumpy ride to the Glosters' rear echelon. Another night in a tent, in a field, then on to the next place until we arrived at Battalion Headquarters of 1st Glosters.

We were checked, inspected and checked again. Given a list of kit and equipment we would require on the line, handing in the remainder to be sent back to one of the rear echelons. We were then sorted out according to rank, experience, specialist knowledge, etc; and allocated to companies. Vic and I were to go to 'B' Company.

There was a pep talk by the adjutant, Captain Farrar-Hockley, and an interview with the commanding officer, Colonel Carne. The interviews were done individually in the CO's office, where Joe Carne shook hands and welcomed each man to the unit, asked a few questions – which showed he had seen our record documents – and wished us the best of luck for our future with the battalion. There were 30 of us. Joe Carne saw every man and made every one feel welcome under his command.

The adjutant gave us a quick but plain briefing on the battalion positions and the situation along our part of the front. Then we were collected by representatives of our respective companies and trudged off to merge with the new environment.

It seemed about two miles to the company positions. We hoofed along winding, dusty, undulating vehicle tracks and narrow footpaths between the hills. The flattish valley bottoms were, or had been, cultivated, but the steep hillsides were covered in long grass, brown and dead from the recent winter. There were also a lot of shrubs and small trees dotted along the hillsides and on their crests, the crests being only a couple of hundred feet high – or even less – near us., In places the trees and shrubs closed up to form dense thickets. The scars of shells and bombs showed here and there. In some places they had caused small landslides which now showed as bare, light brown earth among the vegetation and outcrops of dark natural rock. In the distance we could see much higher hills, and mountains far away.

Major Harding was company commander of 'B' Company. He welcomed the six or seven new faces to his company in a manner which made us feel really welcome, shaking hands with each one and putting friends together in the same platoons as far as possible. Vic and I were sent to No.6 Platoon where we were again made to feel at home. (Especially by the men we were replacing, who would be heading for the UK as soon as we were pulled out of the line.)

The company position was a group of small hills, each platoon had a patch of high ground to itself. As we climbed the narrow track to 6 Platoon's position a brew was put on, which was very welcome by the time we dropped our heavy kit.

We were sent to the same section, shown our trench, where to sleep, our arcs of fire, the breaks in the wire, etc. More ammunition and grenades were issued, then we were briefed by the platoon commander, Lieutenant Peal. He pointed out the other company positions, the Imjin River and one of its crossing places. The hills to the north, beyond the river, were 'Indian country'.

From all the different briefings, and answers I got to a few questions put to the old hands I realised we were not expecting trouble in that sector. The battalion was due to pull back to a rest area within the next few days and, as a 'forty mile' penetration patrol with a lot of tanks and infantry a few days before had found no sign of enemy to the north, there seemed to be no problem.

Nevertheless, a brigade holding a divisional front was pretty thin on the ground. 'B' Company, as right wing of the battalion, had to put out a contact patrol every night to meet a similar patrol from the Northumberland Fusiliers. By this means they covered the *two mile gap* which existed between the two battalions.

Even in the ignorance of youth I remember thinking it wouldn't be so bad against a highly mechanised road-bound army, but the Chinese masses of infantry could flood through the gaps at will. As far as I could see, advancing infantry could ignore our positions and leave us to die of embarrassment.

Also in the ignorance of youth, there is a great faith that those at the top know what they are doing and could of course plug the gaps at a moment's notice.

The British 29th Independent Infantry Brigade consisted of three infantry battalions which, in those days, were Glosters, Royal Ulster Rifles, and Royal Northumberland Fusiliers. Artillery support was given by 45th Field Regiment, Royal Artillery, with their tried and trusted 25 pounders, and 170th Mortar Battery, R.A. with 4.2 inch Mortars. 8th Royal Irish Hussars were the brigade's armoured element, equipped with Centurion tanks, which were then the best tanks in the world.

Further artillery support was available from the huge American 'five-fives' a long way back. Air support was by the US Airforce. Helicopters were a thing of the future in forward areas, rarely seen anywhere, even well away from the front. In fact I saw no helicoptors in Korea in 1951, although I have learned since that some of our wounded were evacuated by chopper.

A Belgian battalion was attached to 29 Brigade at the time, being the Belgian contribution to the United Nations' effort in Korea. The 29 Brigade front was about seven miles. Three battalions were stretched thinly along this front with the aforementioned vast gaps between battalions and smaller gaps between companies. The Glosters were on the left, covering the main supply route (a road running north to south) through the area. Royal Northumberland Fusiliers (RNF) were in the centre and the right wing was the Belgian 'Capitol' Battalion. The Royal Ulsters Rifles (RUR) were in reserve, a few miles back from the front line.

Morale in the Glosters was high, the experienced troops who were the main part of the battalion exuded confidence. Although the all round situation didn't look good to say the least, the troops had great confidence in the brigade, and its commander, Brigadier Brodie. Above all there was an all round confidence in themselves and the other units in the brigade, such as 8th Hussars and the artillery units, as well as complete faith in the ability of the other infantry battalions. The men in my platoon had, between them, seen action in North Africa, Italy, D-Day landings, Anzio landings, Burma and most of the bits in between.

When I mentioned the gaps around us to one old sweat he just grinned and said, 'Don't even think about it, kid, anything happens Brodie will blot those gaps with Artillery, and the Rifles (RUR) will be in there like shit off a shovel to sort it out in no time.'

We two 'green uns' slept well that night. Except when we did our turn on stag (sentry duty), when we listened to the rumble of artillery to the south, the whistle of shells high overhead and watched the flicker of explosions in the hills to the north.

'Harassing fire,' someone explained, 'just to keep them busy – in case they get any bright ideas.'

There was another rather worrying little detail I remember. Vic and I were alloted a slit trench, but it was full of empty ration cans and rubbish.

We had started to dig another hole for the rubbish when we were told not to bother. 'We'll be moving out in a day or two – and there is plenty of room in the next trench if anything happens.'

And so to sleep – hoping the opposition didn't get any bright ideas, like returning that 'harassing fire' for instance.

CHAPTER FIVE

Imjin River

It is worth mentioning at this stage that the modern concept of a soldier in battle, with steel helmet, camouflage smock and slacks, automatic rifle and grenades hanging out of every-where, had no near resemblance to the British Army in Korea.

For a start, only one man in the Glosters wore a steel helmet, don't know who he was, but I heard he existed.

We wore on our heads the common or garden dark blue beret as issued, with our Glosters' badges gleaming proudly. I say badges, because the Glosters wear two badges, one at the front and one (smaller) at the back. The back badge is worn as a battle honour from a war long ago, when the regiment had to stand back to back (surrounded as usual) in order to win the day. Looking at the history of the Glosters, one could get the impression that some situations are habit forming. The good old(?) battledress of World War Two was our field uniform, a blouse and trousers with the added refinement of two buttons on the trousers to hold down the blouse at the back. Heavy boots and canvas anklets finished the picture.

I actually went into action in Korea wearing the above with a shirt and tie.

On the shoulders and sleeves of our battledress we wore our unit and formation insignia. The Glosters' title flashes were the bright red of the Infantry, with the name GLOUCESTERSHIRE in white letters. This was across the top of the sleeve in a slight arc. Below the unit title was, on the left sleeve, the Wessex Brigade sign as worn by the county regiments from the Wessex area of England. On the right sleeve was the formation sign which, at that time was 29 Brigade's black two inch square with a big white circle in it, known to everyone in Korea as the 'Frozen Arsehole'. For some reason I never did get my 'Frozen Arsehole' sewn on.

Our field equipment was the relatively up to date 1944 pattern. (The bulk of the Army in those days still used mostly

1937 pattern equipment with the odd bit of 1908 pattern.) The equipment consisted of two ammunition pouches, supported by shoulder straps and belt, and a small pack carried high on the back.

The dillies who designed British Army equipment up to that date could only envisage how smart it would look on parade. (Or possibly when standing back to back!) The ammunition pouches when full had the effect of keeping one's chest up off the ground at any time when it was the last thing you wanted, and as you dived to the ground the small pack had the knack of pushing your steel helmet over your eyes – or rolling it off into the distance. At least, with no steel helmets we didn't have that problem in Korea.

Our weapons were verging on the antique. The only worthwhile thing we had for the Korean War up to April 1951 was the good old Bren gun, probably the best light machine gun in the world. There was one in every section, so it worked out at one between every ten men. The officers had Sten guns, rather Utility, wartime ones which had been designed primarily to mass produce and use captured 9mm ammunition: not much hitting power and useless at anything over about 50 metres distant.

The 'troggery' were armed with old bolt-action rifles. Great for accuracy at long range – in the hands of this expert or that – at Bisley or some other comfortable Rifle Club on a summer's day in England. But to the trog facing a hail of automatic fire from short range, a bloody liability. At least, to be fair, they were better than spears – just.

The British Army had for many years been the victims of one of the greatest cons of all time. We were told time and time again that well aimed single shots with bolt action rifles would beat 'all comers'. An enemy with automatic weapons could not sustain an attack because they would obviously run out of more ammunition than they could carry, etc. etc.

Before arriving in Korea we were told not to worry about mass attacks by the Chinese, as only one in ten had a rifle. This was basically true enough, but the other nine had Tommy guns, 'Burp' guns or light machine guns. (Brens, like ours but a different calibre). The difference in fire power was such that, I personally, felt it was almost like trying to spit in someone's eye when he's spraying you with a fire hose.

On 22 April, 1951, a few days after I arrived to join the Glosters, we heard reports of enemy troops on the north bank of the river. No one seemed to take this news as anything of note. Life went on as usual around the positions.

We cleaned and checked our weapons every day, sometimes several times if it was wet or dusty. On this particular day everyone was busy cleaning weapons before last light. We also checked and cleaned our grenades, primed all the grenades in the position and made sure everyone had his fair share of the ammunition and grenades which had just been issued.

All these activities, and many more, were carried out in an air of completely normal routine. Vic and I followed the lead of the experienced men around us. There was the usual soldier's talk, the odd joke, friends cursing one another in no uncertain manner, quiet laughter, the loud and lurid curse over some minor irritation. It was the normal British Army scene of quiet confidence. In retrospect, after many years on operations, I have the feeling that things would have been no different with the Glosters 'trogs' even had they known the odds which were about to be flung upon them.

In the evening, a couple of hours after darkness had hidden the hills and valleys around us, the sounds of battle came our way and some shelling of the river crossing took place. We watched the shells exploding and also watched the lazy curve of tracer bullets arcing this way and that as 'A' Company became entangled.

Apart from the occasional long line of tracer which seemed to float gently towards us then pass by with a savage crackle, or thump into our hill, we seemed at first to be merely spectators at an average firework display. This was the first time I heard the Chinese bugles. They were very distant but also very creepy, haunting, eerie. Not the harsh, strong, brassy note of British Army bugles. Something between a hunting horn and a French horn. The notes rising and falling on the night air, competing with the sounds of battle.

The Chinese used their bugles to communicate orders and information, as the British Army had done years before. In this respect they were better off than us, as our radio sets were very unreliable. Throughout the coming battle we would be hearing a lot more bugles, much nearer too.

There was nothing we could do to help 'A' Company as they

were about 3,000 yards from us, well out of support range. Nevertheless, we were on full 'stand-to'. Everyone in his appointed place and ready for action. Well, fairly ready, that is. In my particular trench (next door to our real one) we decided to have a brew of tea or coffee. This was a simple enough operation involving a 'tommy cooker' a mess can of water and a poncho over the top to conceal any light, all in the bottom of the trench.

There were five of us now in that slit trench, which was plenty big enough, but because of the brewing operation Vic was sat with only his feet dangling in the trench at one end, and I was in a similar position at the other end. We were making sure no light showed, also keeping an eye on the slope of the hill.

The first explosion took us completely by surprise. We had seen or heard nothing. In retrospect this was unusual, as on all later occasions the Chinese advertised their presence with a lot of 'hawking and spitting' as well as often chattering like a nest of magpies.

There had been no sound of incoming shells so I was pretty certain it was a grenade. There was no damage, but I found myself lying on top of everyone else in the trench, obviously being last in. Vic had a bit of help, as the explosion partly blew him into the trench. There were yells from the bottom of the trench as they were forced down upon the cooker and can of near boiling water.

Someone in a nearby slit trench yelled, 'Stop those grenades, you're too close to us!!'

Another explosion, closer. Then another, and I noticed something wrong. The British '36' Grenade has a noise all of its own. Those explosions didn't sound right if they were our grenades.

Being on top of the heap – and feeling decidedly exposed around the back end all at once – I looked over the forward parapet and to my surprise saw two or three figures just beyond the wire, about 25 yards away, calmly lobbing grenades at us.

The Bren gun was in position on the parapet right in front of me so, without further thought I grabbed the familiar weapon and plastered a long burst of about 10 to 15 rounds at the dim outlines I could see. A last explosion followed and I could see no sign of the men at the wire.

In the local silence which followed I heard a voice from up the hill behind me shouting, 'Cease fire, stop firing that bloody Bren.'

I thought, 'All right for you Jack, they weren't trying to blow your bloody ass off.'

Within a few seconds the company commander and company sergeant major were at our trench demanding to know why the Bren had been fired. I explained and they looked doubtful, so I don't know where they thought those grenades were coming from. But I was a new replacement and likely to fire at shadows.

They were just about to leave when a hail of fire from a 'Burp' gun chewed up the track just behind their crouching figures. All three of us immediately fired at the gun flash. Then there was silence.

The company commander said, 'OK lad, keep your eyes peeled.' Then they were gone, silently into the darkness, up the hill.

All through this event, which probably lasted about three minutes from the first explosion, the brew-maker in the bottom of the trench had stuck to his post, and now produced two or three steaming mugs of tea or coffee which was shared around. It was when I took my first sip that I realised just how dry my throat was. I also realised that when firing the two or three shots at the muzzle flash of the burp gun, (with my rifle, as the Bren gunner had taken over his own weapon) I had done something by instinct rather than training. I had used the rifle like a shotgun and kept both eyes open, not trying to use the sights (which were useless anyway in the darkness).

Having used shotguns at home, from a very early age it was, I suppose, quite normal to revert to habit when surprised at close quarters. Nevertheless, as I quietly sipped my hot drink there was the worry that I had betrayed my training, not 'done things right' in the first operational use of my rifle. Little did I realise, I would spend a lot of time, many years later, being trained in exactly that type of instinctive shooting.

No.6 Platoon was not bothered again that night, except by stray bursts of heavy machine gun fire from a long way off. I believe one or two of the other platoons in 'B' Company had probes like ours, but nothing serious.

The experienced troops were more interested in their tea

and coffee than anything else and I've seen more flap on training exercises than I saw that night.

Much to my dismay, there were no bodies lying where they should have been when daylight came. It looked like I had fired at nothing, but an old hand found tracks and marks and explained how the Chinese always recovered their men, dead or wounded in the night, when possible. As would we in a similar situation.

Soon after dawn, a solitary Chinese soldier came jogging along the valley in front of our positon. The company commander gave permission and our Bren-gunner fired a short burst which killed the enemy soldier. Three or four of us then went down the hill to collect any documents from the body. I kept a sharp lookout for any Chinese dead further down the slope but saw none. We did see a neat row of six Chinese back packs not far from where the enemy soldier was lying, but did not touch them.

The fighting in the distance became sporadic as the sun rose, the war seemed to be going around us.

We were quite surprised when orders came to pull out immediately, leave everything except our fighting equipment and small packs and move south, up a long spur to higher ground. In fact, Colonel Carne had by then assessed what we were up against and was trying to organise his battalion into a smaller defensive area so that we could still deny the enemy use of the main track, and also prevent companies being over-run one at a time without a chance of support from other companies.

The company moved quickly. A few old hands quickly turned the position into a death trap, with booby traps of all kinds, as soon as we were clear. Our heavy greatcoats were thrown in a heap and I saw grenades being placed among them soon afterwards.

We moved off in a long column with 5 Platoon leading, followed by 6 Platoon, then Company HQ followed by the other platoon.

The company was about 600 yards from its old position when the Chinese started getting among the booby traps. Several of them were gathered around the pile of greatcoats and I saw two or three on the ground after the first grenade blew. They went back to the pile and got caught again before I lost sight of the position.

The spur we were climbing was not too steep but it was long.

Before we had gone far I noticed my friend, the Bren-gunner, with his extra load, was beginning to blow a bit, so I offered to carry the Bren for him. He gladly accepted.

We were right out in the open, on a long grassy stretch, when I noticed a US Air Force Shooting Star, ground attack fighter, going around us in a wide circle. There was a sudden mad scramble to lay out the brightly coloured recognition panels. This was done only just in time. The jet fighter was just stacking up for his attack run when he must have seen the panels. We had no ground-to-air radio communication at company level, and those panels were our only hope.

Before leaving our area the Shooting Star slaughtered a lot of Korean civilians who were running south in the valley at the side of our spur, the aircraft passing so close by that we could see into the cockpit and watch the pilot, intent on his job.

I felt a surge of anger at this seemingly wanton attack on innocent civilians, and no doubt made some comment. One of the old hands turned to me and said, 'It makes everyone sick, but you have to get used to it. The North Koreans have used civvy clothes to infiltrate our lines before now – so nobody takes any chances.'

In the comparative silence which followed the departure of the jet, the wailing of a baby from among the mess in the valley did little to convince me there wasn't a better way to fight a war.

We were nearly at the top of the hill, into a fairly thick cover of small oak, ash and undergrowth, when all hell broke loose up front. Within seconds 5 Platoon came racing back through us, by which time our platoon had fanned out in an extended line and hit the deck, weapons ready.

I still had the Bren gun, so looked for the Bren gunner. Not being able to see him I ran forward to a position where I could see the top of the hill, hit the deck and prepared to give covering fire as required.

The platoon sergeant was nearby and said, 'What the hell are you doing?' I told him what I thought I was doing and he said, 'Well, get your backside ready to move fast, we want all the Brens in the assault line.'

As he said it, Lieutenant Peal, 6 Platoon Commander, yelled, '6 Platoon – on your feet – advance!' and off we went up the hill in extended line.

As we moved forward, Lieutenant Peal told everyone to

watch the top for grenades, and, as soon as they appeared, run like hell under them 'and get among the bastards'. The Glosters had obviously done it this way before, as everyone seemed to know what to do.

I watched the skyline above me and, sure enough, when we were about 25 yards from the top a flock of hand grenades came flying to meet us. I ran up there as I had never run before.

The grenades exploded behind me, and I went over the crest, firing from the hip at any movement I saw. The Bren gun is a beautiful instrument for inspiring confidence (when you are on the right end of it!).Its thunderous fire went before me like a shield of death. A burst of automatic fire came from almost in front of me. Two or three short bursts with the Bren gun either closed him down or frightened him off, and that was the only return fire I was aware of. Glimpses of mustard coloured uniforms among the trees and the half seen silhouettes of two running figures attracted a burst or two each from the smoking machine-gun. Any extra thick undergrowth collected a raking burst – just for luck. Whether or not I hit any enemy at that stage I've no idea. The trees and undergrowth prevented any clear shots, so I just sprayed every movement and kept moving forward. All resistance seemed to crumble before us, until I reached the other side of the position, having (luckily) just changed the magazine and only fired a couple of short bursts from the new magazine.

About ten yards in front of me was a Chinese soldier, we saw each other at the same moment and both fired at the same time. He was standing on a narrow ledge, just below the edge of a cliff, so that all I could see of him was from the thighs up.

He had a Tommy gun and really let it rip. Most of his fire went over my left shoulder, all of mine ploughed up the ground in front of him.

At ten yards' range we emptied our weapons, and both missed. I would have said it was impossible.

He jumped sideways and back over the cliff as I did a fast re-load and rushed forward. By the time I could see him again he was picking himself up from a slide of shale and began to run. I yelled to him to stop as I knew he had no chance (and I was pretty green anyway). Of course he didn't stop, so I kept firing until he dropped.

We had taken the hill in less than a minute and, once organised, found we had no real casualties, only a few slight wounds between the two leading platoons.

I had my 'cap comforter' (a woollen hat, used mostly on night patrols) rolled up and tucked under the shoulder strap on my left shoulder. Amazed to find it full of holes, I realised the Tommy gunner had not missed by much. Likely only one bullet had hit the rolled up hat, but it had gone through many folds.

'B' Company's air of quiet confidence prevailed. The hill position was taken and secured in text-book manner – as if it was just another exercise on a well trampled training area. There was no apparent excitement at our small success, just a business-like determination to do the job, and now prepare for whatever might be our next trick.

Personally, I was full of suppressed emotion. Pride at being part of a unit which could go in with such determined and obviously unexpected speed. Relief that - on my first real assault – I had done most things right, not felt much fear, hit what I had tried to hit (mostly) and got away with it unscathed.

My 'excitement of youth' was, however, soon dampened by the task of searching enemy dead for documents. Dead men are no problem, but they have photos in their pockets which give them reality. Little black and white snapshots of smiling wives, children, parents and grandparents. Happy smiling groups whose smiles will be wiped away by the war. Those good folk had done nothing to deserve this. Ours not to reason why.

The company took up defensive positions on the hilltop, but having only one or two shovels in the company and the hill being mostly rocks, we were unable to dig in. Vic and three others went off with a stretcher, carrying the Chinese soldier I had dropped, and who, riddled with bullets, was amazingly still alive. He died just after reaching the Regimental Aid Post. His comrades were all either dead or had managed to escape the assault.

About that time, as we were preparing to repel the inevitable attack, we heard that 'A' Company had taken heavy casualties and lost their company commander, as well as most of the other officers.

All around us the battle was hotting up. Artillery fire and air strikes were loud and long to the north and west. The haunting, eerie notes of the Chinese bugles were now much

nearer and clearer, mostly to the north and west. I wondered if
the foxes back home felt this way as the huntsman's horn
sounded steadily nearer and nearer.

I had just got down to hard rock, about 6 inches deep, in my
allotted fire position, with the Section Bren gunner and his
number two, when someone called me to the top of the hill,
gave me a pair of binoculars, and told me to let the company
commander know when I could see the American Infantry on a
ridge to the east. I was told they were coming in to help us out
and should be there soon.

Through those binoculars I could see the river and the flat
area to the south of the crossing. The Chinese were taking
heavy casualties in that area, where they were wide open to air
attack and well directed artillery fire. In spite of my situation I
felt sorry for those poor bastards who, like me, were just men
doing their job.

We could hear the artillery firing somewhere to the south
and, in the comparative quiet of what was a fine spring day the
whistle of shells passing high overhead. Then the great flash
and sudden appearance of a fragmented dark cloud of smoke
and dust among the lines of tiny figures running south from
the river. After a few shells the whole scene became hazy, partly
blotted out by smoke and dust.

Then the artillery stopped. The scene cleared. Lines of men
were still running south, towards the battalion positions.

I wondered why the artillery had stopped, then heard the
whistle and howl of the diving jet fighters. Two of them
screamed across the sky, low over the massed humanity, like
rigid silver birds of death. I didn't at first see the napalm bombs
leave the aircraft but I did see them burst.

A hell of burning petroleum jelly, like a line of fire from a
volcano (from my viewpoint), spread through the still running
lines amid a great cloud of black smoke. I watched in
fascination as men ran flaming from bursts of napalm, to stop
and fall in the long grass, leaving a smouldering trail and a little
bonfire where they fell. The Shooting Stars climbed away with
a thunderous roar of their engines and stacked up for their
next run, this time with rockets. We could hear the tearing rush
of the rockets then the sharp crash of explosions as they struck
somewhere among that inferno of smoke and flames.

Again the silver birds climbed across the sky, and again they swooped on their prey. This time the crackling roar of cannonfire followed immediately by the deeper roar of the exploding cannon shells.

By then the aircraft were hidden from us at their lowest point by the clouds of smoke and dust over their target.

A couple of runs with cannon shells then, presumably out of ammunition, the US Airforce went off for their coffee and doughnuts. The whistle and thunder of their engines faded into the distance, and we again heard the rumble of artillery somewhere to the south.

Those readers unfamiliar with the 'ins and outs' of military tactics, abilities, logistics, etc, may wonder why the Chinese attacked us on our hill positions; why they didn't just ignore us and push on with their advance to the south; why they had to buy those hills at such a high cost in the lives of some of their best assault troops.

It was not the hills they wanted, nor was it directly the destruction of the battalion. What the Chinese had to do (if their great offensive was to succeed) was eliminate the observers who brought in the air strikes and artillery fire. Their supply lines could not operate until those people were silenced, and without adequate supplies and reinforcements their offensive was doomed.

The foregoing does not mean the Glosters themselves were not causing enough problems. Their mortars and machine guns were effectively brought to bear on any enemy road movement within reach, but there had to be a limit to their ammunition once they were cut off from the main UN forces. The air attacks and artillery barrages on the other hand, were more devastating and not subject to the same limitations.

While on watch on the hill-top someone called our attention to a section of Chinese who were walking along a track to the east of our hill. The track was on the side of the next hill and, when first seen the enemy section, nine tommy-gunners and one Bren gunner, were walking south, almost towards us. The track could be seen curving east opposite our position then it disappeared into trees to the east. At its nearest point it was about 350 metres from us and much lower.

The company commander gave permission for riflemen to fire at this tempting target, but no automatic weapons were to be used. About five of us, who had a clear view of the enemy commenced firing when the enemy section had almost reached its nearest point.

At the first shots the enemy stopped. One or two went down on one knee. Most just stood still.

Then, to my great amazement they continued on their way, almost ignoring us. I say 'almost' because, apart from the initial pause the only reaction we got was from the leading man who, at the nearest point to our position, carelessly pointed his Thompson in our general direction and squeezed off a short burst of three or four rounds – without pausing in his steady walk.

The most pointed and dramatic 'up you, Jack!' I've ever seen.

The Army and I classed me as a pretty good shot. I re-adjusted my rifle sights and tried again. I tried bloody hard. Not one of the enemy was hit. I suppose we should all have been grateful to the last man of that enemy section for not raising two fingers in time-honoured fashion before he disappeared into the trees about 400 hundred metres away.

An old soldier sitting nearby, who had not fired a shot said, 'Let that be a lesson to you, your shooting got worse every time you missed. Think about it!'

I thought about it, long and hard, to realise I had been beaten by psychology. The enemy had known, as I know now, that if they don't get you with the first shots – when they think they have everything right – then it's unlikely the shooting will improve. If you are lucky enough not to be hit by the first few shots it is most likely the fire will become very inaccurate and demoralise the opposition. A nil reaction to enemy fire makes it very ineffective, a fact which I have put to good use on several occasions since.

It was at about that time I realised we were not up against a screaming mob who relied just on weight of numbers, but were facing some very experienced troops. A lot of them were 'good old boys' who had been around a bit. The Glosters didn't have a monopoly on battle experience in that neck of the woods: a very sobering thought when I again turned the binoculars on the mess near the river and paid more attention to the hundreds who were escaping the napalm, rockets, cannon fire and artillery shells.

Later that day we came under a fair amount of sniper fire. By then I was back in my fire position, there having been no sign of any help coming our way. Someone said the Yanks hadn't been able to break through.

I remember thinking at the time, if there was still only 29 Brigade on a divisional front, against this lot, we were going to have a ball breaking out, if the rest of the UN couldn't break in.

During that afternoon of 23 April, I watched a little bit of Brit 'hard neck' which takes some beating.

One of our platoon was digging a hole with one of the few shovels, right on top of the hill. He was getting steadily sniped at as he worked, and to my amazement was using the shovel to indicate the sniper's 'fall of shot'. Whether or not he was 'telling the truth' I never knew, but at each shot he would stop work, indicate an 'inner' or 'outer', point with the shovel to where the shot had passed him – then carry on with his work until the next round cracked past.

Night came, and 'B' Company was still, I believe, reasonably intact. Before midnight the platoon sergeant took a couple of us down to the 'saddle' east of our position on a 'listening patrol'. We crept down the hillside, facing a full moon, towards a dark line of trees at the saddle. I didn't feel kindly toward the moon that night.

As we reached level ground I could see through the lacework of branches to the track beyond. Trying to focus my eyes through the intervening branches I saw what I took to be a field gun, with armoured shield, wheels and trail standing on the track. As I contemplated what I saw, two huge men appeared. One grabbed the muzzle of the gun, the other grabbed the trail, picked it up and went off out of sight.

It took me several seconds to realise that what I had seen was just two ordinary Chinese soldiers picking up one of their wheeled medium or heavy machine guns, which are more or less the same outline as a field gun, but of course, only a tenth the size.

In less than a minute we had seen and heard enough, and to my great relief started back up the hill. Within a few minutes of our arrival back in the company position our report brought down a hell of artillery shells on the column of enemy troops moving past to the east of us.

Sometime towards morning the mortaring started. I had been asleep for what seemed only a few minutes so had lost

track of time. The first explosion awoke me and I could hear
the swish of more coming. The next few hours were a hell of
noise, screams, shouted orders, crackling machine gun bullets,
then scrambling, panting men coming up the slope spraying at
us with their sub-machine guns and falling in doll-like heaps as
we fired and fired and fired again. The weapons bucking and
pushing into our shoulders as they became hot and smoking.
The haze of smoke, dust and dirt making our targets difficult
to see sometimes. In the bright moonlight our attackers were,
in my case, silhouetted against a light background of moonlight
on the sandy earth and rocks at the bottom of the slope behind
them. Even so I was often firing at the muzzle flash of their
weapons.

Only one, as far as I know, reached the top of the slope in
front of me. I'd had to reload the rifle, and looked up, just as
the clip went in, to see him looming over me, almost on the
parapet. I did the only thing I could and lunged with the
bayonet. He did nothing to defend himself, just stood there. It's
likely he was already dead before the bayonet hit him.

A lot of fuss and bolloxology has been made by various
people at various times about the act of taking human life. In
battle there is no thought, no hesitation, no remorse, no pity.
Only mixed sensations of anger, fear, excitement, exultation –
all vying for 'pole position' as you try to hit the right targets –
like the one who is nearest and firing at you before the one who
is nearer but stumbling forward like a man in a dream. The one
in the act of throwing a grenade before the one who is nearer
but fumbling to pull the grenade pin.

There is also a terrible determination that they will not beat
us, they will not move us – we will gladly kill the bloody lot of
them.

The most dominant, overriding sensation in battle can
probably be summed up in one word, if the opposition is firing
back at you. Apprehension! for your own skin, no one else's.
When it seems certain you will be hit you are inwardly flinching
from the unknown.

So much for the mythical sanctity of human life on the
battlefield, or anywhere else come to that.

I have often wondered how many of the good, kind and
gentle mothers of Dresden, Cologne, Coventry, Leningrad,
London and such places would, given the means, have gladly

blown seven shades of shit out of those brave young lads in the sky above them.

Among the hectic sensations of battle there was also a, perhaps, grudging admiration for the Chinese troops who seemed to exist by the maxim of 'try, try again'.

Not having air support and, at that time, no artillery to compare with ours the Chinese relied not only on a vast numerical superiority of infantry but on the guts and go of the men in their infantry units.

I personally saw nothing for China to be ashamed of during the Imjin River battle, especially when considering these men had probably done a fast approach march of 20 or 30 miles with full battle kit, and attacked straight off the march.

The bugles were very close now but often their strange notes were lost in the welter of sound all around us, only to come through again after a few seconds, clear and close – but still haunting and eerie.

At some stage I realized my right cheek was bruised and aching from firing the rifle which, when it kicked, slammed my thumb against my face. This was due to the rapid rate of fire and continual changing of position and point of aim.

Counting the shots: one, two, three, four, five, six, seven, eight – then worry about reloading another five or emptying the rifle. The panic, if I did empty the rifle, to ram in another clip and start counting again. At every opportunity placing several prepared clips on a piece of brown paper in front of me ready to hand for quick reloading. The rifle would take ten rounds, there were five rounds in each clip.

I noticed the brown paper suddenly had a lot of blood on it, and the clips were sticky when I re-loaded but I have no idea where the blood came from. It wasn't mine.

There wasn't time to worry further than that, but there was time to worry that the sticky clips might jam the rifle.

At the hint of a lull, when we had no one coming at us, there was the frantic activity of re-loading the Bren magazines, pushing single rounds into the rifle to make sure it was full, checking grenades were primed and ready, to hand.

The two 'old hands' with me produced their oil bottles and put spots of oil on the working parts of their weapons. I followed their example, trying hard to remember my training, anxious to get everything right now it really counted.

The mortars were getting air bursts in the trees and sending down a hail of shrapnel, branches and shards of wood. They also hit the ground and those sweating, struggling bodies lying in the open upon it. 'B' Company was being slaughtered, but not in spirit.

An obviously officer's voice shouted: 'Stand fast the Glosters – remember the Back Badge!' and an obviously trog's voice immediately shouted back 'F ... the Back Badge – I want out!'

'I want out!' was one of the current Army sayings, voiced by all and sundry when things got too sticky, boring, or bullshitting, and meant out of the Army rather than the immediate situation. It went along with such sayings as, 'Roll on death. Demob's a bloody failure!'

I was amazed to find myself laughing and heard the laughter of others through the clatter and roar of the battle.

At times I thought there were only the three of us still alive. All the men near us were dead or horribly mutilated, no longer able to take part in anything. When someone came crawling and scrambling to us from behind, I thought we were getting some help. No such luck, they wanted the Bren gunner to go somewhere else to fill a gap in the defences.

So there were two of us now, and no Bren gun. The screams of some of the men lying around us, friend and foe, were terrible, but there was nothing we could do, except try to exist.

Just as first light was beginning to creep through the tree-tops someone brought us more ammunition and a lot of grenades. My companion and I worked as fast as we could to prime the grenades for throwing. A dozen grenades were still in their box and it was as much as I could do to keep my mouth shut when he started pulling pins from the primed grenades and placing them back in their pigeon holes in the box! He saw my amazement and explained, 'For emergencies. When it gets too hot we throw the bloody box and all!'

We had plenty of grenades and the way things were shaping-up it looked a good idea, but I was a bit worried the box might get hit or knocked over before we could use it.

A machine gunner about 200 yards away was picking on me every time I raised up to fire at the troops below. It was daylight, I took out my cap badge, then took off my beret, but still that bastard picked on me. He chewed the rocks to bits and blasted gravel into my face.

Unlike the enemy assault troops, who were completely exposed to our fire at very close range as they scrambled up the steep slope and had practically no target to aim at themselves, the machine gunner was in a good position well hidden, somewhere on a spur of the next hill, north-west of our position, and every time we positioned ourselves to fire at the enemy below we were probably exposed to the waist in the machine gun sights. Each time we fired at the men below I fully expected to be killed. The weight of fire from their automatic weapons, mostly Tommy guns and 'Burp' guns literally chewed everything to pieces all around us. Earth, rocks, roots, grass, branches and twigs shattered in a crazy uproar of crackling bullets, screaming ricochets and shrapnel.

We must have been getting help from other 'B' Company positions but their fire could not be noticed in the welter of enemy fire coming at us. The law of averages was against us. There would be ten or fifteen automatic weapons spraying their contents at us every time we showed – plus that damned machine gun. There was probably a lot of other small arms firing at us from the cover of trees and rocks from which the enemy mounted their attacks, and back to which their wounded crawled, rolled, dragged themselves or were pulled. That was about 60 or 70 metres away, but below us.

Those moments, and many others since, when I threw my life to the winds of chance, come most clearly to mind upon noticing my Army pension is taxed as 'unearned income'! I would love to stand the dreamer who dreamt up that one where any of 29 Brigade stood that day so he could see just how to 'unearn an income'!

Another rush was coming up and I fired from a low position at those along the slope which I could see without rising up, but I knew they were coming up right at me from below as well.

I threw a grenade just over the edge and fired a couple more shots at a few of them who were still coming further along. Then the grenade blew and I jumped up in a rage to nail anyone below me and that bloody machine gunner as well – if I could.

He was a better judge of time than I was, a cooler head, more patient – and he nailed me.

The half raised rifle was slammed back into me and a sledge hammer with a knife on the edge crashed me back in a heap.

I could hardly move. A great numbness engulfed my left side. The rifle was lying near me, its butt smashed away and the magazine and trigger destroyed. Expecting a Tommy gunner on top of me any moment, I found a grenade with my right hand, then, as my left hand wouldn't move, I jammed the rifle between my legs, hooked the grenade pin over the muzzle and pulled it free.

A few feet away the other man in our position was still firing as fast as he could, not realising he was now virtually on his own.

No Tommy gunner came to finish me off, instead, there came a sort of lull. That bloody machine gunner was still blasting away every now and then as if to say, 'I'm still here', but there was a definite slackening of pace for some reason.

In the uproar of sound all around us I was occasionally aware of our own artillery or mortars firing very close support. I know that at one stage shells from the 25 pounders of 45 Field Regiment were falling among the enemy just in front of some of our positions. So close in fact that I worried about being hit by our own people.

I think it was the 4.2-inch mortars of 170th Mortar Battery which caused the 'slackening of pace' to my immediate front. Every now and then mortar shells would land among the jumble of rocks, bushes and trees from where the Chinese were mounting their attacks. At first I thought the enemy had mistakenly hit their own men, then one of the people in the position at the time said, 'Thank Christ for the Royal Artillery!'

Right then I was ready to thank anyone or anything for a bit of a break and, agnostic that I am, envied those who could believe in something I couldn't – and even get some small comfort from that belief. Nevertheless, Royal Artillery or some even higher power, we had a slackening of pace. About then I suddenly felt quite cheerful in the knowledge I had a 'Blighty'. (A wound bad enough to get me sent home – back to Blighty.) How the hell, I thought I'd get out of there, I've no idea.

The other man looked around, relief on his blood-specked face, as he realised we had survived another rush. Then he saw the blood and I said, 'I'm hit.' He stared in disbelief for a few seconds, then crawled under a poncho, and just shook.

A few minutes later Lieutenant Peal came over with more

ammo, saw I was hit and asked where the other chap was. I looked at the poncho, Mr Peal looked at the poncho. How he knew I'll never know in that place of dead and half dead. He called the man's name, pulled back the bolt of his Sten gun, and said 'You have three seconds to get out of there – *one*!'

The man came out like a startled rabbit, stared at Mr Peal, then at me for a few seconds. Mr Peal, said 'You OK now?' The man nodded and resumed his firing position, then carried on as normal as if nothing had happened, and was a damn good soldier too.

Remembering my training, I realised I should have taken out my field dressing and placed it on my chest, in text book manner. But I had a live grenade in my hand with the pin out and couldn't move the other hand, so I lay there in absolute confusion, trying to decide what to do.

The machine guns increased their crackle, but the mortars stopped and I knew another rush was coming, so my problem was solved.

I watched the only other living being I could see, and beyond him the slope further along. Then when he raised up to throw a grenade and I could see the mustard coloured uniforms on the slope again I slung the grenade back over my head and with great relief fumbled for the field dressing. Somehow, the fact that I was likely to be killed in any number of messy ways any second, was as nothing compared with the importance of putting that dressing on my chest as per the book.

Soon after getting the field dressing organised, I had a nerve racking experience. My left arm and hand would not move. I had tried hard – who wouldn't in those circumstances? All one side of my body was numb and felt dead.

Suddenly I became aware of something moving at my side, glancing sideways, I saw an arm raising itself up with the fingers closing, opening and closing. In my dazed state, I didn't at first recognise my own arm. When I did, I tried to control it, but couldn't. At one stage I thought it would claw me, but after a while it fell to my side again.

For some reason, I don't have any idea why, many of us that day had our sleeves pushed up to the elbow and our bare forearms were covered in blood, as were our faces, – from scratches, pinpricks of rock splinters, bullet and bomb splinters.

Also we were dirty from scratching into the ground with our bare hands, and from blackened rifle oil. My arm didn't look like mine.

For what seemed a long time, I lay on my back, gazing at everything and seeing nothing.

The only things I remember, are watching the toothpaste and shaving cream splashing out of my small pack as that bloody machine gun hammered again, and even in the din all around I could occasionally hear the enamel popping from my army mug, still attached to a strap on the pack. The pack was about two feet from my head.

My companion was bobbing up and down, trying to get a look at the steep slope. Suddenly he turned, grabbed the box of grenades with both hands, shook it over the edge then threw it with a pushing motion.

Don't know if it was one of those grenades or one thrown by the opposition but something exploded right on the parapet, covering us with more smoke, dust and rubbish. He shouted something at me, then jumped to the parapet and fired several shots down the slope.

The look on his face when he got down again told me we would be OK from that direction, for a few minutes at least.

Lieutenant Peal came back, and stood over me. 'How are the legs? Do you think you can walk?' I had no idea, I felt completely numb – but I nodded. The machine gunner went berserk, the twigs and branches around Mr Peal were alive with bullets, my mug spun madly on its strap again, dirt and stones flew from the bank.

Mr Peal looked in the direction of the machine gunner, squeezed off a short burst of three rounds from his Sten gun in the same direction, said, 'I'll send a medic – if there is one', turned and walked away, completely unscratched.

A few minutes later a medic came, cut the clothing around my left shoulder and did a quick job with a field dressing. Not mine, it had disappeared – that bloody machine gunner perhaps.

The medic checked me over for more holes, but didn't find any worth patching, said, 'If you find any more holes that are leaking much, give us a shout', and ducked away. He had dragged me back from my fire position, and a few minutes later a couple of men came, dragged me further back and I told

Above Padre Sam Davies holds a service at Glosters' Battalion HQ on Sunday 22 April 1951, literally hours before hell broke loose. The Battalion command vehicle is in the background (*Imperial War Museum*).

Below left MMG Platoon digging in before moving forward to Imjin positions (*Brian Hamblett*).

Below right Setting up a Vickers MMG in one of the positions held before advance to Imjin (*Brian Hamblett*).

Above F80 Shooting Star of the US Air Force. Handled with considerable guts and determination, these aircraft wrought havoc among enemy ground forces, both in the front line and along their supply lines. They didn't give us much time — but we were damned glad of what they could spare (*Royal Air Force Museum*).

Below A B26 Medium Bomber of the United States Air Force. Used singly, as lone night raiders, these aircraft and their crews brought terror, chaos and destruction to the communist supply lines. Pressing home their attacks, usually at a very low level, they were not only taking chances with enemy ground defences but with the rugged, mountainous terrain (*Smithsonian Institute, Washington*).

Bottom Protagonists in the air war over Korea. A Soviet-built Mig 15 used by North Korea and an American-built F86 Sabre in the livery of the Republic of Korea Air Force. Photo taken at the Korean War Museum in Seoul, 1981 (*S. Mercer*).

Left A Lance Corporal in the Royal North-umberland Fusiliers, wearing battledress and the famous red and white hackle above the badge on his beret. The Royal Northumberland Fusiliers wore this uniform, hackle and all, throughout the Imjin River battle (much to their credit — and peril!) (*J.J. Carter*).

Below The people who really suffered. Korean refugees flood south, blocking the roads and dying in their thousands as they try to escape, with their few possessions, from the harsh regime to the north. Also they were safe from air attack behind the UN Lines. North Korean troops, disguised as refugees, had infiltrated UN positions in columns such as these (*Embassy of the Republic of Korea, London*).

25-pounder field guns of 45 Field Regiment, RA, whose accurate support fire, continued when their gun positions were under attack and in danger of being overrun, saved much higher casulaties in 29 Brigade (*Imperial War Museum*).

The main supply route, just south of the Glosters' positions. It is typical of those routes which the Chinese needed and fought so hard for but were denied for four vital days by 29 Brigade. (*British Official Photograph*).

them I could stand up. To my surprise I stood up, and could walk. We moved a few yards into the trees and the next thing I remember is sitting with my back to a tree, staring at an arm and hand lying on the ground in front of me. There were several bodies nearby, at least one was Chinese. I wondered why the arm had been amputated, it didn't look too bad. Why I thought of amputation in that hell where I had already seen much worse, I don't know.

The two men came back, crouching to keep low. 'The walking wounded are being evacuated – come on.' They helped me through a mass of tangled, fallen trees to the edge of the cliff and seemed to be looking for a way to get down. It was the place I had reached when we assaulted the hill the day before, coming face to face with the Tommy gunner.

As we paused at the edge, a machine gun tore apart a small sapling right by me. For the first time I knew real terror. The cliff was about 15 or 20 feet sheer to sloping shale. I just jumped straight out in absolute panic. Landing on my feet, I ran down the slope. Ahead of me was an archway formed between two clumps of alder bushes with an inviting dark thicket beyond. I realised I was on exactly the same route the Tommy gunner had taken the previous morning. All I could think was, 'History repeats itself.'

In blind panic I reached the archway and threw myself through, tripped and fell headlong down the hillside. My head hit something and I went out like a light. Regaining consciousness, I found myself draped over a fallen tree, all panic was gone. I immediately took stock of my situation. The left arm was still useless, hanging like a rope of pain and swinging around freely with every move. The whole of my left side felt on fire. Blood ran from a cut on my head down my face, getting in my left eye and dripping from my nose. Everything else seemed to be in working order.

Getting my bearings, I looked across the valley to the east, where the 20-odd walking wounded were supposed to be going. Seeing some of them going into a small valley about 200 yards away, I knew I had not been unconscious for long.

Before I could move, however, I became aware of a face, staring at me from ground level, about 20 yards down the hill. It was a Chinese face, so I stood still and stared back at the glittering dark eyes. There was no movement and no gun in sight. I glanced left and right, but could see no signs of other Chinese. So it was just him and me.

We stared at each other for several seconds, then I realised something was wrong. He hadn't moved, or blinked. Nothing. A few seconds more and I walked down the hill and past him. He was very dead. A victim of the artillery barrage of the previous night. Then I ran. Past several more Chinese dead, through shell craters, tangled branches and across the valley to where I had last seen the line of wounded. They were moving east, up a small valley climbing directly away from our company position which towered behind us.

I reached the end of the column as the men at the front turned south, to climb out of the valley. They had picked a spot where there had been a landslide, where progress would not be impeded by the scrub and small cliffs.

As the leading men neared the top of the slide a machine gun opened up from near our company position, which sounded like it was being over-run at last.

Men on the slope began to fall. The rest of us rushed on, trying to reach the top where we would be over the crest and into cover of trees. A man in front of me fell, then tried to get up again. Without thinking (maybe), I put my good arm around him and helped him to his feet, then, still supporting him struggled on up the slope. The slope was soft sand and loose rock. It was like the nightmare of trying to run in treacle. Two steps forward and one back.

More men went down, the bullets crackled around us. The man I was supporting was hit again and all the strength went from him. I could no longer support the dead weight and, as he looked dead this time anyway, I let him drop and scrambled on up. He had shielded me from the bullet which finished him. To this day I am not sure if the instinct for self preservation made me pick up a 'shield', or did I help him because he was there? The machine gun fire was from my right, and only my right arm could support him; nevertheless, he stopped a bullet which would have hit me, maybe more than one bullet. As it was, I survived, yet again, and reached temporary safety over the top of the ridge.

At this point in my life I met one of the greatest men I have ever known. Over six feet tall, very broad shouldered, experienced soldier and always cheerful: Corporal George

Baker, from London. Like me, he was from 'B' Company, 1st Glosters. I had probably seen him around but not really met him. He was the man in charge of the walking wounded, charged with the task of getting us out through the Chinese lines if at all possible. George had gone back down the slope and helped others reach the top. He was not wounded and had a rifle, which gave me some hope.

There were now eight of us, including George Baker and a lance corporal who was not wounded, helping George get us out. The lance corporal had a Sten gun with one bullet in the breech and the magazine 'housing' smashed. It was doubtful if it would fire even the one bullet. George had only two bullets in his rifle. We had no other weapons or ammunition between us.

The first thing George did was check the state of the wounded men. One or two extra wounds were dressed roughly. Somone made a sling for my arm with a face veil (small camouflage net), then we set off down the slope to the south.

We had no maps, no compass and no idea of the possible whereabouts of other forces – friend or foe The only map I had seen was a very confused looking thing which Mr Peal had used on his initial briefing. He had stubbed a finger at the various battalion positions and the nearest company position of our neighbours, the RNFs. The only thing I had been able to identify was the Imjin River. We knew the Chinese could be up to twenty miles behind our lines, in great numbers. The artillery were still firing somewhere to the south but it was difficult to judge the range as the hills and cliffs threw echoes in all directions.

I personally didn't have a clue about anything. Had not been in the country long enough to know anything about it. Although I had recently travelled up the road to the battalion area, 'yer average trog' doesn't see a lot to aid navigation when looking through a cloud of dust from the back of a truck.

We were all in the same boat, so it looked best to stick together, head south and hope to get through somehow. I knew which way was which and, with my natural built in know-how, could have found Battalion HQ easily enough but when last seen it had been in a valley, on the road, and there was no way it could have survived that position, so it would have moved or been destroyed. I also knew I would be of no use to Battalion HQ in my state of health so, altogether, there was no point in trying to find it.

Our instructions were to get out, 'out' was south, so south we went. After a while of hurried walking and trotting we came to a road. Just a few yards to our left, to the south, there was a sharp bend in the road and the first two men set off round the bend to check the road. A few seconds later they came galloping back, yelling 'Tommy gun Platoon' and, as if to leave no doubt, a hail of automatic fire sprayed the corner as they left it.

Everyone bolted north up the road, but I stood in some indecision, as I thought it best to go back into the trees, away from the road. The herd instinct took over and I overtook everyone else before they reached the next corner.

The road was in a narrow valley at this point, with cliffs at the sides in places. We turned west off the road into the first valley we came to and ran for some way up a steepish track. After covering some distance up the track we noticed a long line of troops trotting along the ridge to our right. There was some discussion as to whether they were friend or foe. They were too far away to be sure, but I decided in my mind they had to be Chinese – there were too many of them to be anything else! Then we noticed they were turning south around the head of our valley so, as most thought for sure they were Chinese, there was no way out that way. They were Chinese, we found later.

The Tommy gun artists were still following us, the odd burst of fire told us that, so George decided to climb the ridge to our left, which was south anyway. The side of the ridge went up in steps. A steep climb, then a small cliff of rock, then another steep climb, and so on. Some of the cliffs were only three or four feet, others were six or eight feet.

How we got up that hill I'll never know. George Baker was literally heaving the wounded up the cliffs. Not so bad with some, but I was over fifteen stone. At one place George pulled me up by my collar and belt while I scrabbled for a grip with my good hand.

At last we reached the top and the shelter of a young fir plantation. The trees were thickly planted, forming a dense mass, except at the bottom where there was a gap of about three feet between the lower branches and the ground.

The Tommy gun crowd were still persisting. We crawled and dragged ourselves under the trees for about 100 yards, then they ended. Ahead of us was open ground, a shallow valley. On the other side of the valley there were scores of Chinese troops, digging positions and erecting camouflage. They were about 100 yards from us. The Tommy gun crowd were firing the odd burst into the plantation behind us. It sounded like they had spread, and were sweeping through.

There was a narrow track running down the valley, between us and the Chinese positions. The track was only about 30 yards from us. Along the track there came trotting one little Chinese soldier, carrying a long old rifle and bayonet over his shoulder, clutching a piece of paper in his hand. Obviously a messenger, hurrying about his business. George Baker gave his rifle to someone able to fire it, and came out with the quickest briefing – certainly the plainest – I've ever heard. He said, 'I'll go out and put my hands up. If he takes me prisoner, come out one at a time with your hands up, if he doesn't – shoot the bastard and from here on we'll throw rocks.'

With that he stepped out of cover and raised his hands, leaving at least one of us – with great faith in human nature – feeling around in the pine needles for a rock.

The little Chinese looked startled, as well he might, with George up the slope from him looking like 'man mountain' – only rougher. He glanced across at all the help he could get from a few yards away, took the rifle from his shoulder – but didn't point it rudely – grinned, and beckoned George down toward the track. The little man's amazement grew as, one by one, we followed until he had eight comparatively huge enemy soldiers all to himself – his prisoners!

He lined us up and marched us off down the track in his original direction. We had only made a few yards when the first of the Tommy gun crowd broke out of the trees, pointing their weapons and shouting at our captor, who, to my amazement, pointed his old rifle at them and really put them in the picture. I didn't need to understand Chinese to know that! Then off we went again, with our unwounded hands on our heads – and our hearts deep in our boots.

CHAPTER SIX

Into Captivity

Being captured by enemy troops. Made a prisoner of war. Surrendering one's life to the enemy, is the most degrading thing I can imagine. All men being different, there is no doubt that being captured had different effects on different men, I can only speak for myself, state the facts as I saw them. My view only. Nevertheless, I have good reason to believe most of us who were captured at that time 22–27 April 1951 – had very similar feelings and reactions. A deep conviction of having failed. Failed our country, our unit, our family, ourselves – any one of those, or all. In my case, all. Why should I be alive and snivelling to the enemy for my miserable life, when so many had died? What right had I to live when others had died for nothing?

The Chinese had obviously advanced far beyond our miserable little hills, and we had failed to stop them. Was I a coward? If I had done this differently, or that faster, or something else another way – would it have made any difference? To anything? Or was I really surrendering to man's age old instinct to survive? Undoubtedly braver men than I were captured that day.

I went over and over the events leading up to my capture. Should I have gone my own way when we first hit the road? Should I have tried to hide in the fir plantation? Neither had seemed a good idea at the time, so why should they now? They didn't.

The Chinese troops were absolutely saturating the whole area. Acres of them were sat on vast hillsides. Each man about 10 feet from the next, holding a small branch over his head. They were probably invisible from the air.

Soon after capture we were handed over to a proper escort, at some kind of headquarters under some trees. Looking along the hillside, which was fairly smooth and open I could see for about 600 yards (over ½ kilometre) to where there were more

71

trees. The whole open area was covered in troops. Just sitting there, with their little branches. They were spaced about 10 feet apart so as to minimise the effect of shelling or air strikes. They were far less likely to be attacked than were the obvious hiding places, such as woods, ravines, etc. Aircraft and artillery were likely to blast woods, because they afforded cover to the enemy, whether or not any actual target could be seen.

The Chinese uniform was much lighter in colour than ours. It was a light mustard colour when new, but, as it was washed, became lighter and some were almost white. So when sitting in the open with a little local camouflage to break the outline, there was no dark, eye-catching shadow.

Their weapons interested me a great deal. There seemed to be about half with Tommy guns, (the genuine US-made model) or 'Burp' guns, (a Russian sub-machine gun , the PPSh 1941) and the other half had a mixture of rifles. A rifle with folding bayonet seemed most common. This was the Russian 'Simenov'.

The 'Burp' gun was called 'Burp' gun because of its very rapid rate of fire (900 rpm). A couple of quick 'burps' and that was 70 rounds gone – it was empty. Many of the Tommy guns and almost all the 'burp' guns were fitted with drum magazines, which held 50 rounds on the Tommy gun and 71 rounds on the burp gun. Spare magazines were carried in good leather or canvas pouches at the waist, and also, occasionally, in small haversacks slung over one shoulder.

Every Chinese soldier had four or five grenades hanging on the back of his belt. These were what we called stick grenades. They had a handle about seven or eight inches long. Their effect was (thankfully) more blast than shrapnel.

Most of their weapons had a 'plug' in the muzzle, like a cork in a child's pop-gun, with a brightly coloured feather in it and a string attaching it to the weapon. I wondered if this was left in when the weapon was fired and just popped out, as per pop-gun, or if the brightly coloured feather was there to remind them to remove it before firing.

Most of their Bren-guns were carried in leather cases, the shape of the gun, magazine and all, with a zip fastener. The magazines on their Brens were straight, and probably only held twenty rounds.

On their feet some Chinese wore soft canvas and rubber 'hockey' boots, others wore plimsolls, giving them the ability to move around quickly and noiselessly at night, whereas our great, heavy, steel shod boots were a liability on night patrols, especially in the rocky terrain of Korea.

Spare ammunition was carried on the belt and in a bandolier over one shoulder. Over the other shoulder they had a cloth tube, about two or three inches in diameter, which contained their field rations. Their field rations looked and tasted like chicken meal. Adding a little water, they mixed it to a brown paste and ate it cold. Just like that! So simple, not like our flashy rations, but so very effective in the field. The Chinese had been at war for a long time by 1951.

At the Headquarters we were searched thoroughly, but nothing was taken from us, neither documents or valuables. Our treatment had, so far, been fair. We had been given cigarettes (Senior Service) and chocolate (Cadbury's Milk) obviously 'captured'. I think I had two squares of chocolate and was thankful; it was the first thing I had eaten for nearly two days. Little did I realise it would be a long time before I ate again.

We were moved a couple of miles with our new escort, and taken to a small valley, where we found about 30 other British prisoners were being held under guard. These Brits were mostly Glosters, but one or two other units were also represented.

While we were in that valley, we were shelled by our own artillery. Only four or five shells landed near us, but I noticed no one took any action. At least, most of us just sat or lay where we were. Only two men dived for cover. One was killed, the other was severely wounded and died later. They were in among the rest of us, it was as if the shrapnel sought out anyone who moved.

At that stage in the game we were bomb happy, had seen so much it didn't matter any more. We didn't give a damn for bombs or shells. They got you or they didn't. Rumour had it the Chinese had been doping their assault troops. For a start, I'm quite sure there wouldn't have been enough dope to go around, there's no doubt most of them were bomb happy.

There is another phenomenon that affects troops in battle. For the first couple of hours of being shot at, you feel everyone is shooting at just you. After that first two hours (give or take a bit) if no one has hit you – you get the idea no one can. This is not to say you think you are bullet-proof, but you have the confidence to take chances, can afford the luxury of more emotions than pure fright. Real laughter in the face of adversity can do wonders for morale; losing your temper can get your ass blown off!

More prisoners were brought into the valley. They arrived in small batches of sometimes four or five, sometimes ten or fifteen, until there were nearly a hundred of us there. By this time my wounds were a mass of agony, and things are again a bit confused as regards time of day, or even day.

While still in that small valley a Chinese unit of about 50 Tommy gunners passed through. They were very fresh-looking, nothing like the battle-hardened veterans we had seen so far. Their uniforms were newer and cleaner, they were all loud talk and menace. We called then 'Tommy gunners' but in fact I noticed these troops were carrying what looked to be brand new 'burp' guns. The woodwork on their weapons was a highly polished, reddish brown colour, and all had long curved box magazines. This was the Chinese version of the 'Burp' gun, known as the 'Type 50'.

We didn't know it then, but it is most likely these were some of the forward assault troops of the Chinese 65th Army which, in terms of manpower was a second wave of 27,000 men being thrown at the rather battered 29 Brigade. They went through the group of prisoners and took watches, rings and anything they could tear loose. This was no more than we expected, but came as a surprise after the firm but comparatively courteous treatment we had received so far.

I was left alone, having no rings, and my watch was hidden by the makeshift sling. There was a fair bit of caked blood around and I don't think these darlings wanted to soil their sweet little hands. Our guards were obviously terrified of them. We had only about five or six guards at that time, and about forty or fifty of us.

Our guards stood well away from us, spaced in a circle on the slopes around us, so they could look down on the whole group. One had a Bren gun, the others had Thompsons. As more prisoners arrived the guards were increased. By the time we moved out of there, at dusk, 24 April 1951, there were about 30 guards to about 90 or 100 prisoners.

Just before we moved out of that valley we were addressed by an English-speaking Chinese officer who wanted drivers for the few trucks which had been captured, on the pretext that they would be used to transport our seriously wounded comrades. Sufficient volunteers were found and went off under guard.

A few weeks later the drivers rejoined us. They told how they had been conned and forced to drive the vehicles loaded with supplies. They never saw any of our wounded. Although they did not stay together as a group during their driving for the enemy, they all managed to sabotage their vehicles within a day or two, once having found it was a trick.

I don't remember much about that night, except pain, and marching this way and that. There was a thick fog, or river mist and at one stage we got lost from those ahead. We were climbing over paddy field walls, banks of earth, sometimes four or five feet high and I had some difficulty. All I could think was: 'Keep going.' Eventually we located the rest of the column and at dawn were nearing the river. Joining a rough road leading towards the river we met thousands of Chinese troops running south. All had their trousers hanging around their necks. A column of 'flashers'. They had obviously just waded the river and were trying to get clear of the crossing before the fog cleared and the US Air Force came to call.

Before we reached the river we were shelled again, by UN artillery from a long way back. I had lagged behind my friends, so, when everyone dived into the ditches I kept walking down the road to catch up. A Chinese soldier, one of our guards, rushed up behind me and smashed me into the ditch with the butt of his Thompson. He did it for my own good, although I wasn't thinking so at the time, and as the huge shells were landing very close he was putting himself to some risk. That was the only time I was struck like that during my captivity. I did get kicked later, but not hard.

We reached the river and prepared to wade across. With only one hand I took off nothing, as the problem of undressing and dressing was going to take too long. As we waded through the water, which in places, was nearly waist deep, we scooped water into our mouths. I for one, had a raging thirst, we had seen no water since capture.

The banks of the river were littered with Chinese dead, - most of them being downstream – there were some jammed against rocks in the middle, others lying in shallow water and on mud banks. It may have been the crossing place where about 15 men of the Glosters had lain in ambush on the night of 22 April and caught hundreds of Chinese troops helpless in knee- and waist-deep water. The river was about 100 yards across at the crossing. I heard the Chinese had made mass attacks across the river against the Glosters' machine guns, only succeeding when our men ran out of ammunition.

After crossing the river we were rushed away into the hills before the fog lifted. There are memories of woods, with many deep bunkers into which we were jammed like sardines during daylight hours, when the US Air Force roamed free, blasting anything and everything.

We saw the horrific effects of napalm. Men with their clothes turned to ashes, hands like burnt sticks, ears, noses and lips gone. Eyes just wet reddened ash – and still alive, lying where they fell, waiting to die, as there was no help possible.

Every day more prisoners joined the column until it was about 250-300 men. The guards, of course, were increased in proportion. The stories of other prisoners who joined us confirmed our worst fears. The Glosters had been destroyed. It seemed all had been captured or killed. Prisoners from other units, notably the Royal Northumberland Fusiliers and Royal Ulster Rifles were fewer, and their experiences gave hope that the bulk of their battalions had escaped the human flood.

I, who had removed first my badge, then my beret, in the interests of self-preservation when picked on by a machine-gun maniac, was duly impressed and somewhat humbled by the Royal Northumberland Fusiliers who joined us. They were wearing in their headgear the bright red and white 'hackle' of their regiment, which sticks up proudly three or four inches above their beret – and can be seen for bloody miles. I heard one of them saying it would take more than a few 'Chinks' to make them take out their 'hackles' on George's Day! (Saint George's Day is 23 April).

Gradually we built up a rough idea of the catastrophe that had befallen 29 Brigade, the Glosters, in particular. The stories were many and varied from the comical to the horrific. I noticed that any amusing incidents were recounted with relish; the horror stories were not really mentioned, except in the context of some larger incident and there were stories of heroic acts – always by someone other than the story teller.

One good story going the rounds at that time came from the RNF. They told how some of them had been curled up with laughter at one stage of a battle as they watched their cook chasing a Chinese Tommy gunner round and round the cook wagon, waving a meat cleaver, as the unfortunate man tried to clear a stoppage on his weapon. If the final outcome of that situation was mentioned, I cannot remember it.

Some of the Glosters whose position overlooked a few abandoned and disabled vehicles told how a great cheer went up when the NAAFI wagon received a direct hit, blowing it to bits and scattering paper money in the wind like confetti. NAAFI was not too popular with the front line troops on account of the extortionate prices they charged for bringing their goods into forward positions.

One man in the Glosters had been watched in amazement by several men in another platoon as he dashed through very heavy automatic fire at close range to collect ammunition, then ran back into the position with a heavy ammunition box in each hand to re-supply his platoon, which had been cut off and partly overrun.

Another man was seen to play dead, in a position which was partly overrun, until a Tommy gunner jumped into his trench, whereupon he disabled the enemy and used the enemy weapon and ammunition to carry on the war.

Almost everyone seemed to have run out of ammunition before capture. I seemed to have plenty of ammunition, it was the luck which ran out in my case.

Several men of the Glosters told me the same story, at different times. They had been taken prisoner, and were sitting at the roadside, after all resistance by the battalion had been crushed. An obviously senior Chinese officer stepped down from a vehicle nearby, surveyed the wreckage and havoc all around, littered with many Chinese dead, then walked over to the prisoners and said in perfect English, 'You are British.' It wasn't a question, more an accusation. He gazed around at the local scenery again, then said, 'Twelve thousand miles from home – and you fight like this. God help anyone who lands in England.' With that he jumped back into the truck and departed, having paid 29 Brigade, probably, the highest compliment it could ever get from anywhere.

As I was not there, I cannot vouch for the truth of the story, but I heard it several different times, from different men who were there, and the story was almost word for word identical on each occasion. So I believe it.

This was the first indication I had that maybe we hadn't made such a mess of it after all. If the Chinese thought we had been a nuisance to their advance perhaps we hadn't been such a dismal failure. Nevertheless, I could not imagine the British Army, with its proud traditions, looking upon us very kindly.

Very few, if any of us, had any idea of the strength of Communist forces which had been thrown across the Imjin River to destroy us. It had obviously been a big attack involving thousands of enemy troops but further than that the average trog, or even the average 'Rupert', knew very little.

We referred to various places in the battle as 'our first position' or 'our second position', etc; and the place which, a few weeks after the battle was known to all the Free World as 'Gloster Hill' was only known to us for the next two years as 'the Last Hill'.

Only fifteen men of 'B' Company had survived our second position to fight on 'the Last Hill'. The rest had all been killed or captured, except three. One was severely wounded but taken care of by Korean villagers until UN forces returned, about one month later. The villagers had continued to look after the man even after one of them had been executed by the enemy for taking food to him. Which says a lot for the conduct of British troops in foreign lands! The other two 'B' Company men managed to get through the enemy lines a day or two after leaving our second position.

We knew nothing of what happened to the masses of enemy troops as they poured south past our positions. How the attack was ground to a standstill and finally destroyed by UN forces whose time to get into position had been gained by our seemingly wasted efforts.

Not for years after the event did we learn of the great battle 25 miles to the east of our positions, where the Commonwealth 27 Brigade, – Australians, British, Canadians and New Zealanders – put up a terrific fight (during those very same days that our battle raged helping the US 1st Marine Division to destroy part of the Chinese offensive. In fact, the Canadian battalion ('Princess Pat's') was surrounded by enemy forces and cut off for 24 hours, so it must have been a close thing for them too. Luckily for 27 Brigade, although they were heavily outnumbered, there was little more than one Chinese division hitting them, so their situation was not as hopeless as ours.

Had we known of these events, especially the action of the Commonwealth Brigade whose effort against overwhelming odds did much to smash the attack and stop the Chinese advance on their part of the front, our morale would have lifted considerably. As it was, all we had seen was seemingly endless masses of enemy forces which poured over us in apparently unstoppable numbers.

At trog level we knew nothing about having 'achieved the impossible'. That (militarily) we were doomed from the outset of the battle and stood no chance at all.

We had done what we could and been beaten by the enemy. That fact was only too obvious. We were shabby, unshaven, unwashed. Most of us were wounded. We were cold, aching, sore and very hungry. Physically and mentally we had taken quite a hiding, our pride was severely dented, and yet the trog's morale was comparatively good. Not high, but high enough. We could still laugh at our plight and make jokes about it. Spiritually, I realised, the British trog could never be beaten. As individuals, I think we all plumbed the depths of despair, but as a group we lifted the individual's spirits back to group level.

About seven or eight days after capture we received our first food. It was a great tub of white, stodgy rice. Two Chinese carried it on a long pole and placed it on the ground in the middle of the area we were resting in. All the men were starving and there was a mad rush when we realised it was food. A young officer tried to get them to form an orderly queue, and finished up sitting in the tub of rice, which must have burnt his tail a bit, as it was pretty hot.

There was no way the more severely wounded could join the scrum around the rice tub so we just sat and watched. George Baker saw the problem and dived into the scrum to bring us our share.

There was no discipline in that state of hunger, it was every man for himself. Many fingers were burnt in the hot rice – but at least it put something in our bellies. After that first meal there was some hard talking done. It was decided that in future we would organise food distribution so that everyone got his share.

Eating rice, sometimes sloppy rice, was not as easy as it sounds. Practically no one had any spoons or other eating utensils. We had no plates or mess-kit. So we had to do what we could with what we had. Like many of the others I used the inside pocket of my tunic for a plate. George Baker tore it out for me. For a long time I used my cap badge as a spoon. Have you ever seen a Glosters' cap badge? Well, it makes a bloody awful spoon. The only reason I had the cap badge was because I had taken it out when being shot at, and put it in my pocket. My beret was long gone, left in my last firing position.

About five days after capture one of our medics had gone round all the wounded, changed their dressings and cleaned up the wounds as best he could. It was then that I found I had two bullet holes in my shoulder, about two and a half inches apart. There were no exit holes at the back, but my left side was still on fire and the medic guessed at least one of the slugs had glanced off bone and gone down my ribs. He reckoned at least two ribs were broken. The pain stopped him from probing too hard.

Breathing was still difficult but the medic reckoned my lungs were OK or I'd have been 'spitting blood' at some time before now. The worst pain was my left hand. It felt like it was in a permanent state of exploding from the inside. Every heart beat was like a kick on the funny bone. Someone gave me an army glove to put on the hand. It was one of those with a felt back and leather palm. Anything touching the palm of my hand gave me a terrible pain, but, once I had forced the glove on, it felt better, life became more bearable.

Almost every prisoner had some sort of wound. Many of us had collected a lot of shrapnel which, when it went septic, came up in boils which were painful. Probably more painful than when the shrapnel went in. It was in my case for sure, as I had not felt most of my shrapnel when it arrived.

When I looked around at some of my fellow prisoners, my couple of nice clean bullet holes seemed nothing compared to their wounds. One had a lot of shrapnel in the top of his head. I can hear his screams now as his friends held him down and tried to give him some relief, by pulling the worst pieces out with a pair of ordinary pliers. No anaesthetic of course.

Another young lad would give subdued screams and moans for the first two miles every night, until the stiffness went from his wounded leg. He had a large bullet hole through his thigh. Others had smashed hands, smashed wrists, gaping wounds were quite common. Several had bullets in their chests and shoulders. One, with several bullets in his chest, spit blood every night as he marched the first 200 miles. Eventually, he was put on an ox cart, but died within sight of the Prison Camp.

The 29 Brigade prisoners were in two columns for the march north. Two or three times we passed each other and many friends were glad to see others they had thought dead. I was damned glad to see Vic grinning at me the first time we saw the other column. We had not seen each other since he returned to the position after helping carry the wounded Tommy gunner to the aid post. He had been moved to another section, where there had been casualties early on.

Just after seeing Vic and a few other friends I'd thought lost, I saw Colonel Joe Carne. He was standing apart from his column, greeting all the men in my column as they passed. As I approached him I was very surprised when he said, 'Well done, Large. Chin up, we'll be OK soon.'

What a man, how could he remember the names and faces of nearly all his battalion, even to new arrivals like myself – who certainly had not looked like this the last time he had seen us. We now had about three weeks' growth of beard on our faces too. The Colonel was obviously very pleased to see so many of his men alive, as until then I believe he thought the one column were the only survivors.

By day we hid from the UN jets. Once away from the front area we were not put into bunkers any more, but allowed to rest in sparse woods or scrub. Occasionally the jets would strike at targets close by, bringing the war a bit too close for comfort again.

At night we would cover about 20 miles at a fairly fast pace. Sometimes we marched north all night, sometimes east or west and once or twice even south. Roughly every hour, sometimes two hours, the column was stopped for a five or ten minute rest. We never knew how far we were going or what time we might pause for a rest, or reach our nightly destination.

We soon 'twigged on' to the Chinese orders for 'rest' or 'sleep stop'. Someone with the officer in charge of the column would shout an order from the front and this would be repeated by each guard in turn back to the tail end. As we always moved in single file the column was quite long.

A shout which sounded like 'Suselah-Ah', meant 'take five'. The one I always longed for was 'Sweejo-Ah'. That meant we had reached our destination for the night, and would be herded into a small area, to be surrounded by guards and allowed to sleep. Many of us often fell asleep during the five minute breaks. I remember once falling asleep on a pile of loose rocks, in pouring rain. To get us moving again the guards shouted all sorts of things. The only word I can remember sounded like 'Kukali'. Whether this was Chinese or a 'cock-up' of 'quickly' I've no idea.

The guards all had a very frustrating habit of yelling loudly and pointing vaguely with their chin, in oriental fashion, often leaving us guessing what was required – and the wrong guess could bring a torrent of full volume screaming in Chinese accompanied more often than not by a lot of very rude stabbing motions with the bayonet. They had obviously copied, but twisted, an old British Army saying, and thought everyone could understand Chinese if it was shouted loud enough!

Our morale on those night marches was, I believe, quite high considering our circumstances. There was a typical trog's stubborn acceptance of everything and, although there were many of us quite severely wounded, no one – as far as I know – was more problem to his comrades than he could help.

Everyone helped everyone else. I know the human mind tends to blot out the bad experiences and remember the better ones, but through the haze of agony which dominates the memory of that grinding, stumbling trek northwards through the dark mountains and hills of Korea I remember the songs.

The Glosters had been stationed in the West Indies in the late 1940's and (strangely to my ears) there often came floating through the darkness the sound of several voices (some melodious, some otherwise) singing the calypso type songs of the West Indies. Such songs as 'Stone Cold Dead in de Market', 'Brown Skin Girl', 'The Blue Tail Fly', etc.

One song, probably not from Jamaica, I will always associate with memories of that march. I think its title may be 'Two Little Lambs'. One man, whose name I forget but whose voice will never be forgotten, would twist the words a little and sing out: 'We're a few little lambs, who have lost our way'. Then perhaps fifty or a hundred voices would join in the 'Baa! Baa! Baa!'

The sound of that song comes back to me from the steep rocky slope of a mountainside, from the wide expanse of a night sky full of moon and stars, and from the roar of pouring rain on a twisting little track through jumbled rocks. Just when things seemed to be at their worst someone, usually the same man, would kick it off – and lift the dark smother of despair to get existence into perspective again.

Our Chinese escorts varied in their reactions to the songs. Some, usually the older, hardened veterans would take it all with a quiet grin. Others would rush at the column, screaming at us to shut up, and making a lot of threatening motions with bayonets and things. Even there, on that long grinding hoof northward, one of my great hates reared its ugly head. 'Bullshit.' Not bullshit itself, but its consequences. Before leaving UK the units of 29 Brigade had been in the usual position of having to do the average amount of 'bull' which their situation demanded. To the uninitiated it may sound madness but almost every trog in the Army in those days found himself compelled to 'bull' his best boots to a glittering shine. Many 'tools' were used to smooth out the natural wrinkles in the leather so as to produce an overall smooth surface on which to work for hours with cloth, spit and polish (literally). The tools to smooth out the leather were various, such as toothbrush handles, knives, knife handles and – most potent of all – red hot pokers.

A few days before the Imjin battle some of the troops, who had worn out their boots, had changed to their 'best boots'. Having been captured, these men were marching in boots which, a few months previously would have kept them out of trouble by shining brilliantly. But now, those same boots, in their 'bull' damaged state, cracked up under the strain. The leather cracked across the top of the foot and the edges of the cracks cut into men's feet as they marched. I have seen one or two men, whose feet were cut in this way, with blood oozing through the cracks in the leather. As if they didn't have enough trouble already. In the footwear department I was lucky. Having been captured wearing a good pair of 'FP' Boots and two pairs of socks, I had few problems.   One thing which really got me was the cuckoos. Yes, in April, cuckoos go to Korea too. Being a country bumpkin it sounded a bit too much like home, except they sounded like they were laughing at our stupid human misery. Another touch of home was the magpies. It amused me to see they had built their huge nests in the telephone wires, because of the shortage of trees in some areas.

At night the bombers came. They sometimes unloaded their bombs a bit too close for comfort. We had been told that the US Air Force had destroyed every bridge and stopped all motorised traffic between the Korean front line and the Chinese border.

On our first night after crossing the Imjin River we were surprised to see a vast convoy of trucks on a road, all with headlights blazing, coming south. Some of the men thought it had to be the 'Yanks' – 'Nobody else has lights on like that in a war zone!' But the Chinese did. It was at first a great mystery to us how they could get away with it, when American bombers were liable to be along any minute, looking for just such a target.

When we occasionally marched along a road at night we found out how they did it. Every few hundred yards along the roads the Chinese or Koreans had a sentry post. On every truck that moved there was a sentry with a rifle. When a sentry post at the roadside heard a bomber he would fire over the next sentry post, which would fire over the next, etc. until it reached the convoy when, because of the noise of the trucks the sentries on top of the trucks would fire in the air and shout 'Fiji', (which I presume is Chinese for 'aircraft'). Upon which the trucks would immediately switch off their lights and pull to the side of the road, or right off it if possible.

To counter this ploy, the Air Force dropped flares to light up the road every so often, in the hope of seeing even one truck, which might indicate a convoy. We spent many a sweaty time, lying in the ditch at the side of the road, alongside a damn great truck, with a flare hanging right overhead and a slowly circling bomber trying to make up his mind. Once or twice they bombed us. Once or twice they machine gunned us, but by great good fortune they never hit any of our men. (As far as I know.)

At that stage in the game our 'bomb-happiness' had long gone. At least, I know mine had. The rushing whine of falling bombs, the savage, tearing shriek of shrapnel, or the thunderous roar of big 50-calibre machine guns from a couple of hundred feet above me turned my guts to jelly. I sometimes longed for the means to hit back, forgetting they were on 'my side'.

The Chinese were past masters in the art of camouflage. The roads were all dirt, no tarmac. In the dusty dry weather we had on the roads they were a ribbon of nearly white dust. The trucks churned it up in great choking clouds which settled everywhere. Especially on the trucks and their loads. So, from above, the trucks were the same colour as the road, and as long as they kept still, were very difficult to see.

The same idea worked in reverse for the bridges. Most of the bridges between the Front and Red China were intact, just as their Japanese builders had left them. We know because we walked over them. The reason the Americans thought they had destroyed them became obvious. They were covered in pine branches, not like a roof, but laid on the deck of the bridge and lashed to the rails or parapets each side. From the air, the white ribbon of road came to an end at the bridge, and there was a dark gap, matching the river, where the bridge had been.

A lot of the trucks being used by the Chinese were American, captured US Army, GMCs etc. I saw one British truck with the 29 Brigade sign on it. The vast majority of the vehicles, however, were Russian and ran on diesel. The smell of diesel fumes was strange to me, and it seemed nearly always there was mixed with the smell of diesel, the smell of death. The stench of death was everywhere along those roads. For many years after, every time I smelt diesel fumes, I was reminded, and waited for the stench of rotting flesh to creep through. Even now, over 30 years later, I sometimes think of those roads when I smell diesel oil. Somewhere, half way up North Korea, when we had covered about 200 miles in our wanderings, we came to a place known to us all afterwards as the 'Halfway House'. By this time dysentery had begun to take its toll and the column of prisoners was weak and weary.

Ten days after capture a Chinese medical team had come to us, cleaned up our wounds, and put on clean dressings. In my case they inserted the point of a glass tube full of pink 'iodine' in the worst bullet hole, squeezed the rubber ball on the other end and squirted a lot of the stuff into the wound. Some of it came out of the other bullet hole. Then they covered both bullet wounds with antiseptic powder and did a neat bandage job over the lot. Most of the pain in the shoulder eased considerably after that. A good thing too, as no medic looked at it again for two years. The two British Army field dressings had lasted me ten days and prevented any serious infection.

The Chinese were understandably short of medical supplies, considering the casualties they were having at that time. About 50 miles back from the front I saw Chinese wounded, – two on makeshift crutches, one blind among them – making their way north on a track through mountains. They may not have come from the front, and were more likely air raid victims; nevertheless it made one think.

Before we reached Halfway House, I caught dysentery – along with almost everyone else. Being one handed, and now considerably weakened, getting the slacks up and down was some sort of harassment. The guards didn't take kindly to anyone who broke ranks on the march, even when the cause was obvious. By this time we had changed guards a couple of times and now many more had rifles and bayonets, instead of the previous Thompsons. I seemed to spend half of each night's march struggling with my slacks – with an angry Chinese and a flashing bayonet right where I didn't want them.

Two nights before we reached Halfway House, I was in a state of collapse, alternately sweating and shivering and feeling like death. George Baker came to the rescue, half carrying me for most of the night. How he did it I'll never know. Half the night I think I was unconscious and delirious. In the bits that weren't blank, George was there, cheerful and encouraging. Sometime that night I had collapsed during a rest stop. I was brought round by a Chinese officer (not one of the guards) kicking me in the ribs – the broken ones of course. He wasn't kicking very hard, but the pain was horrific. After a few seconds I passed out again. The next thing I remember I'm 'walking' along the road, supported by George Baker again.

There was a very strong suspicion, that if you couldn't keep up with the column, you were shot or bayonetted, so there was a great incentive to go a little further. That night, any kind of death would have been welcome. The next day I improved, and by night had improved beyond all hope. Unbelievably I felt so good, the next march was a piece of cake – I actually enjoyed it!

So, the Halfway House. There were so many sick and weak among us the column had to be rested. Both columns of prisoners were rested there. The sick were separated from the not so sick. After two or three days, those considered fit enough were marched north, leaving the sick at Halfway House, to follow on, about three weeks later. The Chinese told us nothing. So we never knew where we were going, how far, or anything. When the fitter ones marched off we didn't know where they were going, or if we would ever see them again.

The three weeks we rested at Halfway House we stuck to a daily routine. At night we slept in buildings, in my case a cattle shed with muck on the ground, and very little else. At first signs of light in the morning we staggered off to a small wood about half a mile from the buildings. Buildings were unsafe during daylight because of air attacks. We were fed once every day, a small quantity of rice in the evening.

During our stay at Halfway House, we were given one sheet of flimsy paper each and told to write home. None of us believed this flimsy bit of rubbish, like cheap toilet paper, was really going to go back to the UK. Some refused to write, saying it was obviously some sort of Commie trick. Others, including myself, wrote home.

I sat for a long time looking at that piece of paper, weighing up the pro's and con's. If I wrote and told the truth it would be very unlikely to get out of North Korea. Also, if by a miracle, the letter did get home, what good would it do? My family would be worried sick, to say the least. The choice was obvious. I wrote a letter saying I had been slightly wounded and taken prisoner. I was being well treated and not to worry!

The date then must have been late May. On my 21st birthday, 27 September 1951, the letter arrived home, along with another letter written later in the POW camp. It was the first information the British Army had, to say where I was. I had been reported 'Missing'. 'Killed in Action'. 'Missing, believed POW'. So my folks had no idea whether I was dead or alive. The War Office (now Ministry of Defence) requested they send them the letters, certifying the handwriting was mine, etc.

Another thing happened at Halfway House. The Chinese suddenly descended upon us and took away every item of any possible value we had with us. Watches, rings, wallets, pens, even pencils. They made a list for each man and promised it would all be returned 'in good time' – ha! ha! Some of the men saw what was happening, destroyed their watches and pushed them into the dirt, out of sight. I didn't get the chance or would have likely done the same.

The excuse for this caper was that some prisoners had been giving away valuables in exchange for tobacoo from the civil population. This was very true, in fact, as we would do anything for a smoke. I saw a gold watch exchanged for some raw tobacco leaves. The Koreans grew a lot of their own tobacco. Or at least, I presume they did, as we could often get tobacco (*tambi*) leaves from them.

Paper was at a premium for making cigarettes and I have seen men taking leaves from the Bible to roll a smoke. The Padre went right off them when he found out.

One of the most expensive smokes I saw was rolled in a £5 note. I rolled cigarettes in up to ten bob (50p) notes, but drew the line at a 'quid'. Money was no use to us any more. Only some of the American prisoners seemed to value money. We never used it after capture, as far as I know. Just kept what we had, and forgot about it.

Our money was not in local currency but in British Armed Forces Special Vouchers, which everyone called 'Baffs'. The values were the same as sterling but the only coins were plastic pennies, everything else was paper money. Starting at three pence there were notes for sixpence, one shilling, two shillings and sixpence (half-crown), five shillings, ten shillings, one pound and five pounds. There may have been notes of higher value but I never saw any.

Of course this was in the days when money was money, twelve pence to one shilling, and twenty shillings to the pound. I think my pay was about six pounds per week in Korea. The average civilian wage in UK at that time was probably ten to fifteen pounds per week, maybe fifteen to twenty pounds per week. When you consider twenty cigarettes cost one shilling in those days, (5 new pence), smoking even a threepenny note was not good value for money!

The surprising thing about our valuables was that we got them all back. We had been at the POW camp a month or two, maybe three, when one day we were all called to the parade square. We were given the usual lecture about how good the 'Chinese Peoples Volunteers' treated us, then they produced a pile of packing crates, opened them, and inside were our valuables. Each set packed in paper and the crate packed with sawdust to prevent damage. Pickfords would have been proud of them! As far as I know, only one man complained he was 'robbed'. He had a wedding ring returned to him but claimed it wasn't his. I thought at the time he had possibly lost so much weight it didn't fit, or look right any more. But I never found out. The Chinese would have got a lot more value from the whole episode of the valuables if they hadn't been so hard at it with the brainwashing at the time. Everything they did was viewed with the utmost suspicion.

Before leaving Halfway House, some American prisoners joined us. We already had an American pilot there who had been shot down, and was badly burned when he baled out. Now we had about half a dozen more US personnel, another pilot, I think, and one man in particular we called 'Poncho'. Poncho was a tank driver and was very bitter about his unit leaving him to be captured, after his tank hit a mine. He was Mexican-American, short, stocky and very powerful for his size.

Being tallish, my obvious nickname in the forces was 'Lofty'. Poncho, however, always called me 'Lefty' as did many other Americans. 'Lefty' was a common nickname in the US whereas few of them had heard of 'Lofty'.

As is often the case with opposites, Poncho and I became good friends and remained so throughout our captivity, although we did not see each other often, and I have not heard anything of him since my release from the POW camp. He was amazed to hear how things were in the UK. Like most Americans at that time, he thought, for instance, that the police in the UK had very few cars, perhaps none at all, and when chasing the criminal element they would jump on the running board of a passing car, and shout 'Follow that car'. In fact, I once settled an argument between several Americans, half of which were fully convinced that running boards were a legal requirement on cars in UK for the police to use in emergencies.

Poncho was full of funny stories from 'back home', Army stories and hilarious Americanisms. He was very good at 'unloading dead time'. A couple of our boys tried to escape from Halfway House, but were caught and dragged back looking somewhat the worse for wear. One was tied so tightly he had the rope marks on his arms years later.

We spent almost all our time swapping yarns and de-lousing

our clothes. Lice were our constant companions from the first week after capture. At some time during our 'holiday' at that place the Chinese turned a couple of 'barbers' loose on us. They were Chinese, and obviously obeyed orders to the letter. Having undoubtedly been ordered to 'shave the prisoners' faces' they did so, quite expertly, starting at our hair line they shaved every bit of our faces – removing our eyebrows and eyelashes on the way. Had they shaved our heads we would have made a good set of snooker balls, but they didn't touch our hair. No hair-cuts, just a complete face shave!

About three weeks after our arrival at Halfway House we were formed up in a line one night and marched off to the north. No warning was given, we never knew where we were going, or when. Soon after leaving we started marching by day, the risk of air attack became very much less as we moved further north. Somewhere along the way we had to wade a river and were amused to see a huge rusty Russian tank perched high on part of a bridge. The bridge had been destroyed at both ends. The one remaining part – with the tank perched upon it – was tilted at a steep angle like a seesaw.

On that last half of the march, mostly in daylight, we had the feeling we were being paraded for the benefit of the civilian population. Instead of avoiding towns and villages, by using faint tracks through the mountains as before, we now seemed to be forever in front of hostile crowds. Perhaps the change to daylight marching made it seem that way.

At one stopping place a medical corporal was kicked by one of the Chinese officers and made a threatening motion with a stick. He was immediately pounced upon by several guards, his arms lashed together behind his back, then, with his arms out straight behind him he had a rope tied round his wrists and was hoisted off the ground to dangle from the branch of a tree for two or three hours. We watched, helpless to do anything, as he went in and out of consciousness, the dysentery dripping from his feet, and the guards glaring at us over their guns. This was a very isolated incident, and was most likely done to impress the rest of us with the benefits of good behaviour rather than to punish one man for a non event.

Eventually we came to a large cultivated valley with a small town in the centre of it. We marched through the town to its northern outskirts and found ourselves in a suburb which had been turned into a prison camp. No barbed wire, just sentries around the perimeter. As we stopped to survey the scene a big red-haired American left a group of his fellow countrymen and rushed towards us shouting 'The Brits have come, the Brits have come!' I think he thought he was being liberated. There was some yelling from one of the guards – which had no effect – then he was shot, falling dead in the gutter a few yards from us. A British voice from the nearby huts called quietly 'Welcome Home'.

CHAPTER SEVEN

Prison Camp

The POW camp at Chongsung, in North Korea, was the
northern suburb of the town. Between the camp and the main
part of the town was the Chinese Headquarters, housing the
guards, administration staff and all the hangers on required to
run a POW camp. The main road to the north ran through the
camp with no gates, barriers or fences of any kind. A river
flowed north along the west side of the camp. To the east the
ground sloped upwards fairly steeply to hills, backed by distant
mountains. The Land of the Morning Calm can be very
beautiful in that area, and was so at Chongsung.

American prisoners were housed in the northern part of the
camp, British prisoners in the part nearest the Chinese
garrison. Houses in Korea were of simple construction, but
very practical for the climate. All walls were mud and wattle,
interwoven branches with mud plastered on and through, to
form a smooth finish both sides. Usually the inner walls were
papered thickly with newspapers or picture magazines. The
roofs had a wide overhang to keep rain from the walls. Most
roofs were shingle (wooden planks used like tiles). All the
houses were constructed with a strong wooden frame of large
beams and posts. All were bungalows – with good reason.

A cooking fire was below ground level, in a pit about one
metre deep at one end of each building. The chimney from the
cooking fire went through a network of tunnels under the
length of the house floor to a chimney stack at the far end. By
this means the floor of the house was kept warm with very little
fuel and so, as the rocks used in the construction of the floor
retained the heat for a long time, it warmed the whole house.
The floors were smooth mud on top of the rocks and this
distributed the heat more or less evenly. Each house usually
had three or four rooms. Access from one room to another was
usually via an outside verandah along the length of the

building. Most verandahs had raised wooden floors.

There were few, if any windows in the town. I don't remember seeing any in my part of the camp. The doors to each room were lattice, usually from top to bottom, and sheets of thin rice paper were glued to the inside. This allowed enough light to enter the small rooms for normal reading except perhaps in the furthest corners. I saw no glass windows anywhere at Chongsung.

Most of the chimneys, being a long way from the fire, were constructed by nailing together four long planks of wood to form a square sided tube which leaned away from the building and was supported near roof level by metal or wooden struts between chimney and building. I think all the buildings had the fireplace at the north end and the chimney at the south end, presumably with regard to the prevailing wind in the area.

The POW camp had the narrow streets and alleys of its original intended use, as a part of the town, with open areas here and there. Along the streets were monsoon ditches, lined with rocks, to drain the frequent heavy rains. The ditches were usually one or two feet deep and one or two feet wide, but sometimes deeper and wider.

As soon as we arrived we were organised into squads of ten men and allotted our rooms. Everything was 'Communistically' fair. Ten men – one room. In my squad of ten there were at least three of us over six feet tall. Our room was a small one, six feet six inches by six feet. Our lice were all related, and likely suffered from inter-breeding. To make things worse, I could only sleep on my right side as my left arm and ribs were still a mass of pain. As there was no room to sleep on our backs, and if one turned, all turned – there was an obvious problem. It says a lot for the men in that room that we had few harsh words in several months of those conditions. Another squad nearby had a room almost twelve feet square and there wasn't a six footer among them. We were not allowed to change rooms and had to be in our own room to be counted at any time of the night.

The British contingent was organised into two companies, each of three platoons, each platoon had up to ten squads with up to ten men in each squad. Each company had its own Chinese company commander and staff who worked in the company office, which was shared by the Chinese platoon leaders and 'instructors'. The Chinese platoon leaders, one for each platoon, could not speak English, but gave the orders. The Chinese instructor could speak English and interpreted for the platoon leader. He was really a fairly well-trained political commissar whose English was often not that hot. In many cases – thank goodness!

Each company had its own cookhouse with one Chinese cook helped by two or three prisoners. Daily routine in the camp started at 6 a.m. A Chinese platoon leader would emerge from the office on the dot of six and blow his whistle loud and long. Then he would walk around the huts blowing the whistle from time to time. As soon as the whistle sounded we were expected to move quickly from our huts to the company parade ground to be counted.

After this initial roll call the Chinese company commander would usually give a short speech, interpreted by one of the instructors, ticking us off for some minor laziness, etc, or praising us for some achievement in the cleaning or wood collecting jobs. Then we would be told what our next trick was. It was usually to march up to the main parade ground to join all the other prisoners, British, American and any other nationalities for a long and boring political lecture.

The lectures were never a known quantity. They could last an hour or all day. We never knew when we would return to our huts. If we did get a short lecture it was pretty sure we would be instigated to do political study in our rooms. The Chinese would roam from room to room trying to get a political argument going, listening outside the rooms to check if we were discussing the correct subjects, etc., and generally making a nuisance of themselves when the last thing we wanted to do was talk politics. Sometimes the whistles would sound again and back we would go to the main square with all the other prisoners for another few hours of political patter. Those whistles ruled our lives. I still hate to hear whistles.

The officers were put in a separate camp, on the other side of the town, with American officers. After a week or two in the camp, all ranks above corporal were moved to another camp near the officers' camp. I believe there were roughly 600 British prisoners counting all ranks, officers, sergeants and other ranks at Chongsung.

At a guess I would think the American prisoners numbered about three thousand. Some of them had been captured in

1950 and, by the time we arrived, a lot of them were in a pretty bad way. There were only two British prisoners in the camp before the arrival of those captured in April 1951. They were two men of the RUR who were caught in an earlier battle. One of these had been wounded before capture and by the time we found out he was there, – two or three weeks after our last group arrived – he was at death's door. Some of our people approached the Chinese 'Instructors' and the man was moved in with the British contingent, where his friends from the RUR took him on, and worked hard to achieve a good recovery. We had a very small sugar ration at the time and every British prisoner must have given a small proportion of his ration at some time or another to help someone who was 'going down the pan' as we called it. Dying.

When he first came to us, the man from RUR was deaf, blind and totally crippled. Within a month, thanks mostly to other RUR prisoners, he could see and hear. In two months he could walk again. All through our captivity the British prisoners helped each other. The fit ones helped those less fortunate. No man felt alone for long. It just happened, without any apparent organisation.

The American prisoners had been captured before us. The winter in captivity had taken its toll, not only in lives but in the morale of the survivors. They were dying at an alarming rate. I certainly did not spend my time watching burial parties, and was not particularly interested in the problems of the Americans, but one morning I did notice 25 bodies being carried up 'Boot Hill' from the American camp. When I mentioned what I had seen, no one seemed to think it out of the ordinary. There were burial parties on the hill every day, but I never did count again.

Some of our friends who had gone to 'D' Company were missing, but we had high hopes they had escaped to the UN lines after the battle. We knew, from some of the 'D' Company men who were captured, that some of their company had managed to break out, although, when last seen by at least one of the prisoners, they were being shot at by American tanks. Some of the 'D' Company men who were captured had turned to take on the pursuing Chinese rather than fall under the guns of their allies. Years later I learned that 35 men escaped capture or death. None of my friends was among them.

Forward slopes of the 'Last Hill' (Gloster Hill). Although several weeks after the battle, the scene is typical of infantry hill positions at that stage of the war: open holes to fight from, covered holes to sleep in, wide-open, well-worn paths show complete UN air supremacy (*The Gloucestershire Regiment Museum*).

Hill 314, taken by 'B' Company, 1st Glosters, on 23 April and held against repeated mass assaults until the company was ordered to withdraw to the 'Last Hill' on 24 April. Photo taken from 'Last Hill' (*The Gloucestershire Regiment Museum*).

This tank, of 10th Philippino Battalion Combat Team, was knocked out by the Chinese and, blocking the road, prevented help reaching the Glosters. Photo taken a few weeks later after the tank had been moved (*British Official Photograph*).

A Centurion tank of VIIIth King's Royal Irish Hussars (8th Hussars) crossing the Imjin on 7 June 1951, six weeks after the battle. The courage of 8th Hussars and the skill with which they fought with their Centurions were major factors in the successful withdrawal of the bulk of 29 Brigade (*The Tank Museum, Bovington*).

A study in expressions — some of the men who reached safety after the battle (*British Official Photograph*).

Lionel Essex of 'B' Company, 1st Glosters, was wounded in the head, left eye and both legs (one of which was broken). Captured, interrogated and left to die, he was picked up by UN forces 27 days later, thanks to some very brave Korean villagers, one of whom was executed by the enemy for helping him (*Imperial War Museum*).

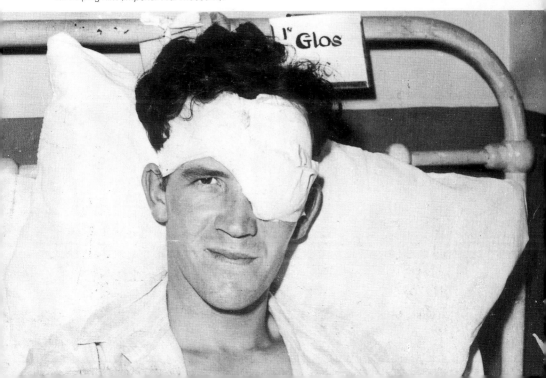

Above A recent photograph of the memorial erected on Gloster Hill (the 'Last Hill') commemorating the Battle of Solma-Ri, the official and local title for the Glosters' part of the Imjin River battle. The pupils of a nearby girls' High School tend the site and maintain the memorial in their spare time (*W.N. Thomas*).

Below left In September 1951, 70 Battery, 45 Field Regiment, Field Artillery, whose amazingly accurate support fire had kept down the odds on our doorstep during the Imjin battle, fired their 100,000th shell of the Korean War. To mark the occasion, Brigadier Tom Brodie, commanding 29 Brigade, turned up to fire it (*Peter Farrar*).

Below right A typical Korean house of the type POWs were housed in. Apart from large towns, almost all houses were like this. Note the paper on the inside of the lattice door, the wide overhanging roof to keep the rain from the mud walls, and the wooden verandah connecting the rooms, which rarely had interior doors (*The Gloucestershire Regiment Museum*).

Three or four weeks after I arrived at the prison camp, Vic went down with malaria, which he had contracted in India, while with 1st Wiltshires. It went the usual course of up and down, with the downs becoming worse until Vic was eventually carted off to the prison camp hospital.

The hospital was an old Japanese temple, on a hill overlooking the town. In 1951 it was not really a hospital – just a death house. No doctor, no medicine, no hope. There was straw on the floor to sleep on, which was the only thing better than the rest of the camp.

A week or two after Vic went to the hospital we were told he had died of malaria. About a month later, two Americans came looking for Vic. When told he had died of malaria, they said he certainly had not. They said they had been in the hospital with Vic and he had recovered from malaria after about ten days, had said he was returning to the camp, picked up his kit and walked out. Vic was never seen again. He had just disappeared. There was no mileage for the Americans telling us he had walked out if he hadn't. So we had to believe them. The Chinese we questioned knew nothing except Vic had died of malaria when they told us. They said they had received a report from the hospital.

Brits did not die easily. As far as I know only three British prisoners died in that POW camp. There may have been one or two others. Not counting the man who died of wounds just before we reached the camp, I can only remember three. There was one, I didn't know his name, or what he died of. There was Vic. Then there was 'Old Pop', who was fortyish, older than most of us. He had been wounded, he had malaria, tubercolosis, beri-beri, dysentery and of course malnutrition. 'Old Pop' hung on with that lot for weeks. It became almost the first question of the day – 'How's Old Pop?

Eventually he died. It had to happen, the odds were beyond even 'Old Pop's' fighting spirit – but it said a lot for those around him who had done their damndest to keep him alive, never giving up hope.

Just across the street the American prisoners, by contrast, had what we called the 'three whole days and no candy disease'. They had, as mentioned earlier, been prisoners longer than us, had suffered the rigors of a North Korean winter in those conditions. But we could not understand how young men, many with the badge of the US Marine Corps on their jackets, could just sit down and die. No wounds, no specific illness in many cases, but no will to live either.

We know that, in some cases, if an American looked like he was dying his room mates would be playing cards for his boots, his wedding ring, his wallet – anything. In many cases, after he died, he would be propped up so the rest could draw rations for him.

There was one huge negro who carried a heavy bag around with him all the time. Other Americans told us it was full of gold teeth. When I saw the bag, it was soft cloth, or canvas, with a string around it to keep it closed. The round bulge in the bottom was the size of a baseball. I never saw inside the bag so I'm not sure what it contained, but – knowing the conditions in the camp at that time – I'm pretty sure.

It is likely no one will ever know how many died at Chongsung. Once when the subject came up, I remember someone saying it was over 800. I think that is a very conservative estimate. On the one day I watched the burial party they had 25 bodies. Perhaps it was an exceptionally bad day, at the worst time, I don't know, but the burial parties went up that hill every day for three or four months after we arrived at the camp. After that it tailed off until there were very few burials in the last few months of my captivity.

Soon after we arrived at the camp we were lectured on the Chinese Peoples Volunteers, and their 'Lenient Policy'. We were told none of the Chinese in Korea were regular soldiers, they were all civilian volunteers. Because we were basically working class people, not responsible for the war in Korea – having been duped by the Capitalist Imperialist Warmongers of Wall Street, etc. – we were eligible for the 'Lenient Policy' as applied to prisoners of war. That was why our lives had been spared, and we were being so well treated. We had not really been captured, but liberated from our Capitalist masters by the Glorious Chinese Peoples Volunteers – who were even now marching forward to victory in the south. (I remember thinking it sure enough looked like it when I left the front!)

Having put us all in the picture, one man was appointed 'squad leader' of each squad. He was appointed by the Chinese irrespective of British Army rank, age or anything we could pin down. The squad leader was responsible for collecting rations and organising the squad to clean its room and immediate area. He was also responsible for the good behaviour of squad members and the squad as a whole. Not an enviable position.

The next trick had us rolling in the aisles. Each squad was issued with a question paper and ten blank sheets, one per man. We had to study the questions then write our answers on the blank sheet. It was the questions and possible answers which raised a laugh. One question was: 'Why should Rockefeller have all those millions of dollars? The answers were very varied such as 'Why not' or 'He worked hard for it' or 'Somebody had to pay the workers' etc. Near the bottom of the page: 'Who started the Korean War?' Answers: 'North Korea' or 'Commies', one I saw said, 'You bastards'.

They had a day or so to sort that lot while we grinned and swapped jokes about the answers. Then the laughing stopped. The lot of us were ordered on parade and the gist of the lecture which followed was 'Running Dogs of the Imperialist Warmongers of Wall Street etc. are not eligible for the Lenient Policy and will be moved to a camp where the Lenient Policy has never been heard of. In future all men will put their real names on their answer sheets, the squad leader will be held responsible for every sheet being correctly answered and returned to the office. Squad leaders who fail in their duty will be punished.' Many answer sheets, except the funnier ones from the first batch, had been used to roll cigarettes, or in the on-going war on dysentery. Most of those returned to the Chinese bore those famous names like 'Mickey Mouse', 'Tom Mix', 'Kilroy', 'Aunt Sophie', etc.

Now the pressure was on. There was no way we could risk getting our own people punished. The hate of all things political started at that point. The British Army is a non-political organisation. Loyalty is to the Crown, representing the Country, irrespective of political parties. Hardly any of us knew anything of politics in those days – before the present mass media situation proved there's little to pick between the lot of them, except there are the extremists and the rest of us. Once the political nuts had us over a barrel they never let up. They appointed a further 'hostage' in each squad. He was called the 'monitor! It was his job to collect, distribute, read and discuss all the political documents issued and return them safely to the office.

We did the absolute minimum to get by without causing reprisals. The 'instructors' would go from room to room and try to discuss politics. Some of us argued with them, not realising this was just what they wanted. On the political scene they could make black look white – and prove it!

I argued, and continually had any point turned against me, until I went right down to basics, where I had firmer ground to stand. Then they were stumped, got angry and I had to back off once or twice, or risk trouble. The first argument I nearly went too far with, was with the 'Hedgehog' (because of his haircut). He had proved black was white again and I said, 'You are a political instructor'. He agreed. I said, 'You can prove to me – politically – that black is white. OK I'm a soldier, you take a rifle and give me one. We'll walk up yon hill from different sides and see which bastard walks down again.' I didn't think it was that bad, but the 'Hedgehog' nearly had a fit. For a moment I thought it was jail for me. But he calmed down, and stamped off, still in a rage.

They didn't like it when we mentioned how the Commies in Russia had helped Hitler smash Poland. It was a fact they couldn't dodge. I also got close to 'hot water' when I likened the Chinese operation in Tibet to Hitler's annexation of Austria.

But the one which really had them running for their red books and never did get answered properly, yet didn't raise any tempers – was the simplest. I told them I had lived under *Real* Communism – in a barrack room – where everyone was on the exact same pay, had exactly the same kit, treatment, facilities, etc. After a year or so, some had nothing, some had a little money saved, one or two had bought bicycles. Why should those who spent all their pay on beer and cigarettes be jealous of those who were now better off? Should they now share the wealth of the barrack room between all? Communism in its true form cannot work because all people are different.

They said this was simplifying the question out of all proportion, but could not come back with a real answer.

The Chinese were completely convinced they were right. That South Korea had started the war. That all the people living under the 'Capitalist Yoke' were being exploited every which way and were itching to be educated and liberated. They tried very hard to educate us, but failed miserably. The more we learned of Communism, the better we could shoot holes in it. Eventually, after about eighteen months, they gave up. There were still lectures and propaganda talks, but we sensed their hearts weren't in it any more.

One thing I could always understand about the Chinese. They were immensely proud of their country, as any man should be. They said the name 'China' almost with reverence. They were brave men in Korea, as we knew only too well. I had no hatred for the Chinese. They were honourable men who did what they had to. Communism was like a disease in them. It did a lot of good in China, only because things were so bad before. But the nature of the Chinese people is too strong to be held in rigid shafts for ever. When they step from the shafts and are given their head to go, as go they must, China will be truly great, in every way!

Political lectures became a daily routine. Usually the whole camp, British and Americans, was herded on to a great parade ground, told to sit down in lines, then harangued, first in Chinese then in English.

After a few weeks someone had the idea of stools, so we were all issued with a stool to sit on. This consisted of a short log of about eighteen inches, with a twelve inch plank nailed to one end. These stools made it more difficult to sleep during the lectures, easier for the roaming instructors and platoon leaders to keep an eye on our attentiveness. Like most of the men, I finished up with an amazing ability to appear really into a lecture, but always have my mind elsewhere – or switched off altogether. I think some of us could be effectively asleep with our eyes open.

This has proved a problem ever since. As soon as someone starts a lecture – I start to switch off! Unless the lecturer is very good and makes it very interesting, there is no way I have a clue what it was all about at the finish.

Some of the lectures went on for hours. Starting at seven in the morning and not finishing until sometime in the afternoon. I have even seen a couple of Americans, who had presumably marched to the parade ground, manage to die during a lecture. (Obviously bored to death.)

At some stage in our march north – I think it was just before 'Halfway House' – I found an old rusty cigarette tin. It was a '50 Woodbine' tin, round, about three inches deep and two and a half inches in diametre. After cleaning with sand etc., it became my food and water can. I could collect my food in it and found I could balance it on my injured hand, which protruded from the sling, to eat a relatively comfortable meal. Thanks to the glove I had no trouble now with hot rice.

When we first arrived at the P.O.W. camp there were a number of Puerto Rican troops living with us and getting rations from the same cookhouse. No matter how I complained I got one fill of stodgy rice in my can, while the little Puerto Ricans were filling their American steel helmets. They must have been getting about twenty times more food than we were, but Communist justice was one can each. I longed to find a five gallon drum.

After we reached the prison camp, rice became a luxury we didn't see very often. The staple diet was sorghum, sometimes millet. Sorghum has round grains which swell when cooked, as does rice, but it tastes foul, comes out pink with blue and mauve patches when cooked. Millet was some sort of birdseed. That too tasted foul, even worse than sorghum. Our diet was boosted by a ration of sugar. This started when we first reached the camp and was issued every ten days. The sugar ration for ten days was, at first, five level dessert spoons. This was increased to ten level dessert spoons, by easy stages, over two years.

After a month or so at the camp there was great news. We were to have vegetables to go with our sorghum or whatever. In the event it was turnip tops, or something similar. We called it 'greens'. The greens were boiled with a lot of water in a boiler tub, and at first were pretty few and far between. But the water had a certain taste and helped with the sorghum. By the time the greens came along, some of us had beri-beri. This is a condition caused by malnutrition. The first signs are puffy feet and ankles. If nothing is done about the diet the puffy condition climbs quickly up the legs. After a week or so the swelling becomes painful, searing hot pains shoot up and down the legs, especially the lower parts. No one seemed to know the cure. The Chinese were sympathetic, but seemed to have no idea what caused beri-beri or how to cure it. I'm quite sure they would have solved the problem if they could.

If nothing is done to arrest the condition it progresses up the body until, I am told, you drown, it stops your heart or gums up the works somehow. You die anyway. We tried exercising, running and walking etc. This only caused a lot of pain.

In my squad we had a great idea. I was the only one with beri-beri at the time, so, full 'soldier's logic' was brought to bear on the problem. Everyone had ideas which I tried one after the other – unsuccessfully. Except one idea I drew the line at. We had all decided the swelling must be fluid, so one idea was that I could cut a couple of holes in my feet and just drain it out. I said that was definitely the last resort stuff – and anyone could try it when I got too swollen to move. But to make damn sure I couldn't move first.

Kicking that idea around, someone had a brainwave. The obvious answer – why hadn't we thought of it before? All I had to do was sleep with my feet up – drain it out of my legs and piss it out in the morning – simple.

So that night my feet were propped up and I spent a more uncomfortable night than usual, not having room to sleep on my back of course. In the morning, shouts of victory when my propped up feet were seen to be greatly reduced. Then they saw my head. I couldn't see out of the swelling for about an hour after sitting up. The things I did for medical science.

Comforting words like, 'Jesus Christ, look at his head' and, 'Blow your nose – it'll come out your ears', and one who really tried: 'It's mozzie bites on his eyelids – they were murder in here last night' – did nothing to quell the panic I tried not to show. Afterwards I saw the funny side, but at the time I wondered what damage could be done in my head by this creeping, horrible fluid.

Our salvation came from a little bloke in the Medical Corps called Janman. He had read about beri-beri somewhere way back, and felt that somewhere in his mind he knew the cure. He racked his brain for weeks, from when the first cases were seen, among the Americans. One day Janman cracked it. The word came around like wildfire. 'Eat greens, eat anything green – grass, nettles, any damn thing.' Everyone with beri-beri immediately went on extra rations of greens from the cookhouse. I ate grass, nettles, leaves and weeds of all sorts. We went through the camp like locusts. Beri-beri was gone within a couple of weeks. By the time young Janman got it right I had fluid up to above my waist and was in some considerable pain, mostly in my legs. Walking was becoming difficult. I was afraid to lie flat – knowing it could creep up in the night.

Another problem which affected quite a lot of people after

about eighteen months in captivity was 'night blindness'. Although they seemed to have their normal eyesight during daylight, the moment the sun set they were almost totally blind and had to be led around by those of us who could see. No doubt it was another 'vitamin deficiency' problem, which was solved soon after their release.

I did notice that the people who suffered the problems of 'beri beri' were nearly all men who had not been in the front line for long before capture. People like myself (perhaps a bad example) who had been used to a lot of rich food – lots of eggs (at least five or six per day) bacon and bananas, etc, in Hong Kong, followed by terrific Aussie rations in Japan – had gone from that excess of nutrition to almost nil, in one sudden step. Whereas men who had been in the field for months had been on much less nutritious field rations and the change of diet was not so extreme.

There was a lot of beri-beri among the Americans, due perhaps to their rather lavish field rations. Our name for the 'disease' which killed many of them – the 'Three whole days and no candy disease' – was, quite possibly, a good diagnosis, except it should have been 'Three whole months –!'

Almost everyone had dysentery. Men had to rush out in the night several times, heading for the latrines. The latrines consisted of a big trench with poles around the edges. We sat on the poles 'Gloster fashion'. Back to back. One man who never made it to the latrines became famous as the 'Phantom Arsehole'. Almost every morning we would find where he had struck, usually on the small parade ground between the huts and the latrines, sometimes on someone's verandah or in the street.

All the budding Sherlock Holmeses got to work on the problem, but the Phantom Arsehole eluded all for many weeks. Then we had our first mail from home, and the next morning when we turned out, we found the Phantom Arsehole had not only struck on the parade ground but, having put an envelope to good use, had in the blackness of the night – left his name and address in the middle of the strike. So ended a sad mystery, which had whiled away many an empty hour and caused more laughs than it probably deserved.

I had at least one letter in that first batch of mail. Unknown to me at the time, Ann, my future wife, was writing five letters every week from the time I was first reported missing. Using all sorts of addresses which were sent to relatives of those missing, and some from common sense, she bombarded North Korea with a deluge of mail – and some got through. During my captivity I received about 100 letters. The vast majority were from Ann, but I also received a few from my mother, and one or two from other relatives and friends. So about 400 of Ann's letters went missing. She wrote to some strange addresses before a proper address was supplied by the Chinese.

On several envelopes my address was, my number, rank and name, 1st Glosters, POW camp, North Korea, c/o Peking. Two or three letters were c/o Budapest. When people said to me 'Two's up' (after you) on the sports page' they really meant it. Ann used to put in the odd snippet of sports news – to fill up a page, no doubt. Although there were doubtless sporting events of great significance taking place in the outside world, the sort of thing I got was more likely a few results from 'Third Division South', a new name on the bike racing scene or when so-and-so beat so-and-so at cricket in the local village league. Nevertheless, these snippets were usually home news to someone in the camp.

Compared to most of my fellow prisoners I had a lot of mail. Why so much mail was stopped from reaching us I have no idea. Where was the mileage in it?

To have the best chance of getting my letters out of Korea I always gave the impression we were being well treated and there was no problem except waiting for an end to the war. One of my theories on getting letters out, was that if the outside world knew we were there then the Communists would have to account for us one day – if Communism was to be given any credibility at all in the free world.

Letters from home were, for many reasons, one of the greatest morale boosters we had. Just an envelope with our address in familiar handwriting would do wonders, even had there been no letter inside. In autumn of 1951 we started collecting timber from the mountains. The timber was for our own use, for cooking and heating during the coming winter. The 'wood details' as they were called, were an immediate success for many reasons. They got us out of the camp for much needed exercise on fresh ground. We found edible fruit growing wild in the mountains and supplemented our rations.

The exercise was great for those planning to escape, and allowed chances for local area 'recce' for quick routes into the mountains.

At first light in the morning a company of camp guards would double march off into the hills to surround the area of the wood detail. About an hour later we would march out into the appointed area, sometimes where trees had been felled and cut into lengths for carrying, sometimes into an area where we had to search for dead wood. I found my ability to carry anything heavy was severely restricted by my injuries, and was afraid of being taken off the wood details. But the Chinese showed a bit of common sense and I was allowed to carry smaller loads.

I was still suffering considerable pain, especially in the left hand. Little did I think that some welcome pain relief was at hand – due to the wood details. Due to the wood details and Poncho, that is. The Brits and Americans had now been separated properly, with guards posted at intervals between us. But with a bit of careful watching we were able to nip across the street without being noticed. Especially if a diversion could be fixed to keep the guards busy. One day, it must have been sometime in late October, early November 1951, I heard Poncho had been looking for me in our part of camp, and sure enough a day or two later he was back – looking secretive, but like the cat who stole the cream.

He got me out of sight of any Chinese and out of earshot of anyone else then he said, 'Lefty, you still got the arm problem?' I nodded. 'O.K. now listen – your problems are over – I got the weed'. He looked at me like he'd just explained everything. Seeing the blank looks he got on with it. 'The weed, you dummy! It grows in the Goddam mountains – and I found it – it's the best Goddam pain-killer ever sent down the line!' Mental picture of Poncho rubbing my arm with some sort of herbal concoction. I obviously looked doubtful. 'You can't get hooked on it – if that's your problem. And it's the real McCoy, I've tried it myself. It's just like back home, there's no big hook, it's OK. You can take it straight or mix it with tobacco – a couple of pulls and Powee! No pain!'

The beginning of understanding twitched in my thick skull, but I didn't really understand all this about 'hooks' and 'straights' – sounded like boxing talk. Poncho's patter always did take some to keep up with, but now he was excited. Full realisation only came when he pulled out this bundle wrapped in paper, about the size of my fist, and showed me what I had to do with the brown leaves inside. Poncho racked his brains for my sort of language then said slowly, 'It's marijuana, the weed. You smoke it. It's non-addictive, I promise you.'

My complete ignorance of the whole drug scene was such that if Poncho had just told me what it was, marijuana, and not told me how to use it, I would have very likely tried to make tea with those leaves. I don't think I would have trusted anyone else in that camp to tell me about using the 'weed'. Certainly not my own people, who knew no more about it than I did. But Poncho I could trust absolutely in that department. Knowing something of his background, his knowledge of such things could be taken for granted. And he looked the part, anyway!

After Poncho went back to his camp, I found a quiet spot and remembering his instructions, built a 'straight' smoke. Then I made one of my ordinary cigarettes and went to the cookhouse for a light from the fire. I lit the ordinary tobacco cigarette then, finding the squad room empty, I sat down and lit the straight weed. At the first lungful of smoke from the weed my arm blew up. The pain was terrible for about four or five seconds, while I held my breath in panic. Then it went. I thought well, 'shit or bust', nothing ventured nothing gained, and took another pull. This time, no increase in pain and within a few seconds all the pain had left my arm, for the first time since being wounded. The relief was really fantastic. Unbelievable.

Remembering Poncho's instructions, I extinguished the weed. Just sat there wallowing in 'no pain'. I felt a bit stupid, and couldn't stop grinning. I had plenty to grin about right then, apart from the effects of the weed – the pain was gone. I could feel like I used to feel, when I had two arms and nothing hurt.

The pain I had suffered during those first six months of captivity, cannot be described or put into words. Sometimes it was worse than others, but it was there to be lived with all the time. I tried hard to shut it out of my mind and after several years have had some considerable success. Practice makes perfect, but in this case I now know there is not enough time for practice to make perfect in my lifetime.

Anyone who has had the usual problems of rolling cigarettes with paper and loose tobacco may pause to wonder how I managed with only one usable hand, coarse newspaper and very rough tobacco. Ability and expertise are often the children of necessity. I could roll a cigarette with one hand as fast as most people could with two hands. Not long before Poncho brought his great gift of pain relief, I had managed to move the little finger of my left hand for the first time.

Two of my friends in that place, both of whom had been PT instructors with the Glosters, had given advice and tried many ideas to try to ease the pain, and get the arm to move. The biggest problem throughout was the pain. Any attempt to move the joints in the arm or shoulder produced screaming agony in the shoulder and palm of the hand.

I had discarded the sling soon after arriving at the camp. By then the arm was set in the position it had been held by the sling. By late autumn 1951, the arm and hand had lost almost all flesh. The elbow, wrist and finger joints were like knots in a rope. The finger nails of that hand never grew. It looked dead, and was not a pretty sight.

Those two men in particular, who had some knowledge of fitness training etc. and who helped many others in the camp, some less fortunate than me, did all they could to help. Their most valuable contribution, it seemed, for months was hope. Although the arm continued to deteriorate they kept at me to keep trying to move it, or any part of it. What made me believe in them was the pure logic they came out with. Such as, if it hurts there is obviously feeling, if there is feeling it cannot die. If there is feeling, the nerves must still be connected, therefore it must be possible to move it – or parts of it – when the nerves have recovered sufficiently.

They told me to get a stick and try to hold it with both hands. I wrapped the dead fingers around the stick as best I could after much sweating and agony. On and off for weeks I spent hours trying to make those fingers curl on their own. I put all my will-power into that hand. All it gave back was pain.

Eventually it happened. The little finger moved. I had to stare hard to be sure the pain wasn't making me see things. I was holding the stick in my right hand, palm up, and it was lying across my left palm, the fingers not touching it. I was trying to squeeze the stick with both hands, as my friends had told me – trying to get 'sympathetic movement'. It worked, all those months of struggle paid off when I saw that slight twitch – and realised it was in time with the squeeze with my right hand.

I rushed to tell the two PT instructors and found them together. They watched the finger perform, then told me not to rush things, but to work on it every day until I could move it enough to hold the stick. Then go back to them so they could show me the exercises which would build up the rest of the hand and arm. They agreed we had a great breakthrough, but cautioned against too much too soon. I did as I was told to the letter. Within a week I could touch the stick with my little finger and the finger next to it began to twitch on cue.

The next exercise involved the stick, a length of string and a small rock. I held the stick as before, with one end of the string tied to the middle, the rock tied to the other end. Then rolled the stick with my right hand and gripped with my little finger – slowly at first – to roll the rock up to the stick. Soon after that great step forward, my shoulder began to work again. The elbow took longer to get going and, in fact, took several years to completely straighten.

The hand and arm put a little muscle and flesh on, but was still a scrawny claw after my release. Just before I was released the finger nails began to grow again.

It is likely that the 'weed' helped in my recovery, although, by the time Poncho brought it, my hand was just about moving in all joints except the forefinger, which took much longer to recover and was a pain unto itself. Being able to 'switch off' the pain occasionally brought a great relief to my life, but I used the weed sparingly, as I never knew how long it must last, or if there were any unknown side effects. After using it for about a month almost every day, I stopped using it for about two weeks to see if there was any craving for it. The only craving I got was for relief from the incessant pain, so I felt secure with Poncho's pain killer.

The weed was not as tame as it is painted in modern life however. Several experiences convinced me it would be lethal back home. One experience in particular is worthy of mention, and underlines the previous use of the the word 'lethal'. Due to my crippled arm, I was often asked to carry 'illegal' odds and ends around the camp when the Chinese would have noticed other people and asked awkward questions.

One day, when I had just had a session with the weed, I was asked to collect a large empty bottle from one point and move it to another. I was quite used to the weed by then and didn't give it a second thought. Off I went and collected the bottle, put it inside my jacket, under the left arm, and set off. My route took me right past the Chinese Office and a couple of officers were sat on the verandah steps. The usual guard was standing a few yards from them, eyeballing everything that moved. So I thought it unwise to pass too close in front of the office, and with that thought in mind decided to walk up on the opposite 'side-walk'. This would involve stepping over the rather deep monsoon ditch at the side of the road. Fifty yards from the office, I went towards the side of the road, this would look perfectly natural as I intended to look in my room as I passed, and stop there a few seconds if the Chinese were showing too much interest.

At this stage I was quite normal, had made a logical appreciation of the situation and made plans to move accordingly – something which everyone does on streets anywhere. I approached the monsoon ditch with the intention of stepping over it as I had done hundreds of times before. The ditch was about four feet deep and about two and a half feet wide, with good solid built rock edges. Two paces from the ditch, it moved away. I hesitated, knowing it couldn't possibly. But there it sat, just a ditch, only now it was about five paces away. I couldn't do anything stupid, like throw a rock to see where it went, without risk of attracting attention. So I sauntered on casually for a few yards then tried again. The ditch sat where it should until, again I was about one or two paces from it, then off it went. I stopped, looked up and down the street. No one was taking any notice of me, the ditch, or anything else in particular.

I tried again. Same thing. By this time I was not only getting worried, but getting a bit close to the office to start doing anything stupid. So I turned around, strolled back down the road and had a go from a different angle. That bloody ditch bugged out again. There was an open patch between the huts, no verandah just beyond the ditch. I passed the spot and made my plan.

Turning again, I came back toward the open patch. Just the ditch between me and open ground. I watched the Chinese, the guard had his back to me, the two on the verandah were chatting and laughing. I got the ditch lined up – ran and jumped as far as I could. When I took off I was about two or three feet from the ditch. I must have cleared ten or twelve feet – and landed smack in the ditch. The bottle under my jacket smashed against the rocks on the far side.

In the air I watched that bloody ditch keeping in front of me as it moved again. Jumping out of the ditch quickly, I glanced up the street, the Chinese were all looking, so I grinned and walked slowly towards my room. Everyone lost interest before I got to the room.

There were two or three of my room-mates in the squad room and they could see at once something was wrong. All gathered round and helped collect the glass as I slowly opened the jacket. There was very little blood, and I peeled off a heavy army pullover. There was then one piece of glass stuck to my ribs. I tried to brush it off. It wouldn't move, so I held it between finger and thumb and pulled. Then there was blood. It shot out like a tap turned on – all over the floor, and I had a long sliver of glass between my finger and thumb.

Someone jammed a towel against the wound, but it was obvious we needed real help. We went to the office, across the street. One of the Chinese officers took us along to the medical room, which had not long been opened, and a Chinese nurse stitched the wound. Another Chinese officer wanted to know how it happened, so I said I fell in the monsoon ditch, and there was a piece of glass on the side of the ditch. The officer who took us there said he saw me getting out of the ditch, so all was explained.

It was not the wound that bothered me. That ditch had appeared to move. After that I rarely used the weed, except at night. At night it was especially useful for a good sleep.

The point of all this is, the weed would be lethal to a pedestrian on city streets, let alone to a car driver. It can have sudden unexplained effects similar to drunkenness, but with drink you can feel the amount you have drunk and act accordingly. With the weed, it's different somehow. The weed can pick on one particular object and blow your mind with it – as in my case, with the monsoon ditch. I am quite sure to this day, that ditch was the only thing which acted wrongly. The rest of the world was plain cold sober, and looked exactly as it should. That doesn't happen with drink. I should know, I've been there enough times too!

The stupid people who condone the so-called soft drugs of which the weed is one – to use Poncho's words – 'Think with their balls and talk through their arseholes.'

CHAPTER EIGHT

Prison Life

The weeks and months dragged slowly by in the prison camp. Apart from our immediate worries of survival there was the background worry of what was happening in the outside world. News given us by the Chinese was, of course, heavily dosed with propaganda and consisted of grand denunciations of the 'American Imperialist Aggressors and their Running Dogs' who were 'hell-bent' on sabotaging any peace proposals made by the 'Peace Loving People of China and Korea' – as representatives of the 'Peace Loving Peoples of the World'.

There was always the possiblity that a Third World War would break out and we were constantly reminded by the Chinese that the first move in the event of global war would be the removal (by the Russians) of 'that American aircraft carrier off the coast of Europe'. Meaning, of course, the UK.

The war in Korea seemed to have no end in sight. We realised it could drag on for endless years. The possibility of never seeing our homes and families again was a stark reality.

The Communist authorities tried hard to get prisoners to chant anti-American slogans. No one would. On one occasion we thought our friends in the American camp had cracked. A company of them were marching back to their camp, through our camp, from the lecture ground. They were all chanting, as they marched, 'We wanta Peace – We wanta Peace'. Then the punchline came – at full volume – 'A piece of ass!!' It gave us all a good laugh although, I must admit, a 'piece of ass' – in the American context – was pretty low on our list of priorities right then. Chinese–American relations, which looked on the up and up at the start of the chant, were noticed to hit a new low when the Commies eventually caught on.

Conditions improved gradually, with the Chinese trying to get the maximum Commie propaganda out of each step. The more they tried, the more they failed, of course, such is the British nature.

Every few weeks someone would 'go over the hill,' but every time they would be dragged back within a few days to be jailed, having achieved very little.

One of the Commie 'gimmicks' which our captors tried hard to instigate was 'self-criticism'. If anyone misbehaved, or was lazy, did not do his job as well as he should etc, he was expected to stand in front of the assembled platoon or company and denounce himself in no uncertain terms. We were told 'self-criticism' was the basis of good discipline and hard work throughout China, and all Chinese Forces in Korea practised it 'diligently'.

Perhaps it was, and perhaps they did, I doubt it, but with us it was a dismal failure in its intended purpose, giving us more laughs than the Chinese thought good for us. Escapees were paraded to criticise themselves in front of the whole camp. One man in particular, who was 'away over the hill' several times was paraded in the usual manner on the camp parade/lecture area. He was led up onto the stage by several guards. His head was bowed, chin on chest, (most unusual for him), he looked decidedly 'roughed up'. A long list of his 'wrong doings' was dramatically read out by an interpreter. Then he was pushed to the fore to criticise himself for his terrible behaviour (escaping). He stood for a few seconds, head still bowed. A great silence fell over the hundreds who had been paraded to hear his criticism.

Then he raised his face to us and said, in a strong loud voice, 'I bin a ba-a-ad boy!'

The grin which then lit up his face put us all into convulsions of laughter. His popularity with the Communist element hit an all time low – for which he undoubtedly suffered – but that kind of morale booster was much treasured by the Brit and American trogs.

In early 1952 I had an idea to solve the great problem of where we were. All we knew was that we were in North Korea, about 40 miles by road from another POW camp at Pyoktong, which was on or near the Yalu River. The Yalu River forms part of the border between Korea and Manchuria, a province of China. The town we were in was called Chongsung, or Chungsong, or Chongsong, or etc. (There are a lot of towns with similar names in Korea).

Part of the propaganda war was the issue of newspapers, from China, The English language edition of the *Shanghai News*. In that paper there were often rough maps of Korea, showing the place of this Chinese victory or that UN atrocity. I copied those maps on to bits of scrap paper and gradually built up a fairly accurate master map which showed a lot of interesting things. Other odd maps and things came my way, always adding to the total picture. There still remained the one great problem, our actual location.

The propaganda kit came to my aid again. The *Shanghai News* was very precise in its reporting of 'Cowardly Indiscriminate Air Attacks by the American Imperialist Aggressors on Helpless Civilian Populations' anywhere and everywhere in Korea. The date, the place and – most important – the exact time of every air raid was faithfully reported. So I became an air raid watcher. Air attacks on distant towns were often visible at night. I watched and waited for the first glows and the sparkle of distant flak in the sky. Then I logged the date, time and rough bearing.

To get the bearing, I had a spot near our room where I could lay a cross of sticks on the ground. This was lined up on the chimney of the next hut, which was in line from that spot to the Pole star. From knowing true north, and looking over my cross towards the air attack, the rest was easy. The problem was the waiting. The *Shanghai News* arrived at our camp about a month late on average, besides which we didn't get every copy. There was sometimes a gap of a week or more, sometimes only every other copy over a period of several weeks. So after each air raid I had to wait a month before I could hope to match my date and time. But it worked, I fixed my position in Korea – and it was a long way from where a lot of people claimed it was. My position fix was confirmed by British Intelligence after my release, by which time I had confirmed it several times myself, with more fixes on distant air raids.

During my air-raid watching activities I saw three or four aircraft shot down. The only raids I could get a fix on were at night, and it was often a lonely vigil on cold winter nights when no one with any sense was out of his room.

On one occasion I saw a bomber caught in a cone of searchlights. It was a long way off but I could see the aircraft diving and turning to escape. Then it seemed to give up and flew in a straight line to the south. I didn't see the night fighter, but the stream of tracer from its guns came from the darkness above and behind the bomber, leaving a flicker of fire on the aircraft. The fire gradually grew larger until the bomber dived steeply to the ground where the flash of its ending threw the western horizon of mountains into sharp relief. Others I saw were hit by anti-aircraft fire from the ground defences and went to earth in a long, curving, flaming dive. The childhood experience of watching German raids on Birmingham and Coventry helped with judging the distance to the point where the raid was taking place, giving me more information for my fixes.

When we were first captured, we were casually interrogated a couple of times. An enemy who captures the whole damn unit, including the CO and the whole orderly room set-up, is not much bothered about interrogating ignorant little trogs. Once, somewhere before we reached the POW camp, I faced an interrogator who (in retrospect) probably just wanted the practice. It was most likely at Halfway House, I'm not sure. He asked a lot of military questions about my unit. How long had I been in Korea? What towns in Korea had I visited? What other units had I seen? etc.

He tried to be very sharp, brisk and vaguely threatening. It made me nervous because I couldn't see where it was leading. It didn't lead anywhere, just suddenly stopped after about an hour. I knew nothing anyway, having been in Korea such a short time before capture.

In the POW camp there was at first a sort of 'documentation interrogation'. Seemed like they were building a picture for the records. Nothing much at all. Then Myrtle came. She was suddenly put in the platoon I was in, as platoon 'instructor'. Her English was pretty good, she was aged about 25 to 28, 5 feet nothing in her heavy fur-lined Army boots and had the average to good Chinese looks. She had a reasonable sense of humour and could 'give and take' with quite a bit of ribbing from the assembled platoon. Individually she was very direct, correct and something else I cannot define. Rumour had it she claimed to have been a 'good time girl' in Hong Kong, and wore a red dress at one time. She didn't tell me that.

Myrtle had been with us for about two weeks when the problem started. One night after dark, one of the Chinese staff shoved open the door to our room and said 'Ladgah'. Most Chinese had problems with my name. When I sat up he said 'office'. I pulled on the boots and followed him.

In the office there sat Myrtle, at a big table facing the door. She told me to sit on the bench on my side of the table, facing her. I had been to the office like this before, but in daylight, to face a man. This was different from the start. She said nothing. Thumbing through notes on the table in front of her, glancing up at me occasionally – for all the world like a very strict school teacher, looking through a terrible exam paper. Then suddenly after several minutes, 'What is your Army number?' I told her. 'Why is it different from all the others?' I told her. 'Why are you lying to me?' I said, 'I'm not lying, there must be other Brits with Regimental numbers here, ask them.' Myrtle stared hard at me for a long time, then, 'You do not tell me what to do! You do not lie to me again.'

I think the number was an excuse. A point to start at. The questions went on, and on, and on. 'Where does your father work?' 'Where does your mother work?' 'Has your father got a car?' 'Was your father in the Army?' 'Why did he make you join the Army?' 'Why did he not stop you from joining the Army?'

I cannot remember all the things I was questioned on, or perhaps I should say I can't remember anything I was not questioned on! That first session went on for nearly two hours. The next night it started later and lasted about three hours. After a week I was dreading the night and that voice at the door, 'Ladgah, office'.

I was 21 years old, sitting across the table from a good-looking woman half the bloody night, and frightened to even smile out of turn. If I had something to hide I could have boxed clever (maybe). But I had nothing of use to them, and couldn't understand why all this questioning. I thought it must be a kind of brainwashing to make me answer all questions automatically then suddenly they would pop the real one. But there wasn't a real one. How could there be?

Then Myrtle started on one of my friends and we took it almost in turn for a week or two. We never knew whose name would be called when that door opened. The worst stage of that episode came after three or four weeks. It wasn't the night she played 'kneeses' with me while she asked the questions – with her pet tommy-gun artist standing casually with that yawning muzzle an inch from my right ear. It was the night she did the knee's bit and sent the guard off to get some cigarettes. I was certain there was someone else involved. She had sent the guard away for cigarettes before and I understood enough to know what she told him, but that was before the knees bit. She often gave me a cigarette during the calmer bits, when we were more like two people working on the same problem.

A few nights after that worst one it stopped. She never called us to the office again. We had both had similar experiences and were both at a loss for a reason. We were both convinced there was someone watching from the next office.

A couple of other interrogation sessions put me right off the whole Commie set-up. There had been a few escape attempts and I think they were fishing for the next one. I was hauled into the office for no particular reason and had a nasty half hour or so, full of questions about who were my friends in the camp and what friends had I got outside the camp? Then there was a sort of casual reference to the fact that he knew my parents' address, and my girl friend's address. Oh and by the way, did I know how strong the British Communist Party was? How dedicated they were to helping their comrades against the Imperialist Capitalist Aggressors, etc? 'They probably have your parents' address, and I'm sure they will have your girl friend's address. Now shall we start with the first question, all over again?'

I thought then of my Mum and Dad, in their lonely house, miles from anywhere. Living their honest, hardworking lives far from the worries of Commie or Fascist bastards who should be wiped quietly from the face of the Earth. I swore to myself then, that if a Commie so much as knocked on their door, I would dedicate what bit of life lasted, to blotting every bloody Commie in England. Perhaps in the long run it would have been better if a few doors had been knocked on. Half a dozen of us could have saved the country from the 'Recession' and a couple of million from the dole queues.

Oh yes, that's another thing which was promised for us in 1952! They conceded the UK could not be taken over by the same means of revolution as most countries, due to its 'peculiar' political set-up. But we were promised that the UK as we knew it was doomed. It would be achieved by control of the trade unions and infiltration of a political party. At the time we laughed at the thought. 1977 was the rough deadline, and I can imagine how other people's laughter, like mine, sounded a bit hollow by then! I blame the top people 'on my side', who must have known all this long ago, and did nothing about it. Not so long back, the extremists, just as prophesied all those years ago, looked to be almost destroying my country. Did all my friends die for nothing over the years? Was all that agony and suffering they went through just a laugh for someone?

Why were we required to sell our lives dearly? To defend or attack a far distant hill in a far distant land, slaughtering other good men in the process – just to see these dumb clots hand our country over to the totalitarian extremists in the end?

Many years ago I was paid about £6 per week to shoot Commies in foreign lands. Right now I'd do it for nothing, if someone would declare 'Open Season', here in UK.

Other men had the 'veiled' threat thrown at them, but I doubt if the British Communist Party was aware of any of it, and I never heard of anything happening back home.

Getting out of the camp was no problem. It was quite easy to slip past the sentries in the night. The great problem was in moving across a well populated country for hundreds of miles without being seen. After the Korean war I was told not one UN prisoner escaped from North Korea.

Twice I went up on the hill east of the camp to have a smoke in freedom. On both occasions the corn was high in the fields, giving plenty of cover at night. In retrospect it was stupid, at the time it was great! As soon as we arrived at the camp, we were given a tobacco ration, for which we were truly thankful. A cigarette or a pipe can be a great help against boredom. The snag was paper. There was no paper with which to make cigarettes. I think we all tried to be pipe smokers at one time or another, but very few stuck to it. In my case it was more fun making the pipe than using it.

The rooms with several layers of newspaper stuck to the walls were a boon. We peeled the walls and used that to roll smokes. Every bit of paper we could lay our hands on went up in smoke.

A lot of ingenuity was used to make darts and dart boards, and many teams were formed. A darts league got under way – then the Chinese decided darts were a dangerous weapon and banned them. Decks of playing cards were made from old cardboard, bridge became a favourite pastime for many months.

Before darts were banned most of us belonged to one or another of the teams. The team I joined was called 'The Barley

Mow', after a pub in Cheltenham. All the members were from Cheltenham area. The team captain, 'Robbo', was one of the great comedians of the camp, and could be relied upon to knock a laugh out of any situation. His bright blue eyes almost always had a merry twinkle in them but, on occasion, he could make them look empty, vacant, wild. I don't think the Chinese knew quite what to make of him.

One game we played a lot was 'Aggis' or 'Haggis', I'm not sure which. This was like golf without the clubs. We set out a course of holes, got a pebble each and tossed it from hole to hole as per golf.

Once organised at the camp a couple of our people set themselves up as 'camp barbers'. They cut hair and gave us a shave once in a while. 'Robbo' started a craze which lasted for months. He had his head shaved 'down to the wood' except for four small patches, one back, one front and one each side above his ears. The four patches of black hair were in the shape of Heart, Club, Diamond and Spade. On another occasion he had his head shaved except for a six-inch pigtail which hung down the back, and to which he tied a little bow of pink ribbon.

Another of Robbo's inventions was the Griff Hat. The kapok hats issued with our winter uniform had ear-flaps which were usually buttoned on top, but in very cold weather we let them hang down to cover our ears. Robbo fixed a piece of thread to one of his earflaps, so that, when pulled by his hand in his pocket the flap would rise up to uncover his ear – so he could better listen for griff (information). Or shit-house rumours more likely. Some of the guards were completely mystified by the 'Griff Hat', and possibly more than a little nervous of it, in combination with the vacant eyes.

After Robbo started the mad haircuts most of us followed suit, with many 'mohicans', 'hot cross buns', 'Friar Tucks', and a host of other weird and wonderful designs. It was all good for morale and raised many laughs.

Robbo was also one of the chief exponents of 'invisible sewing', etc. Several people were quite good at it. They would sit on their own with a garment on their lap and go through all the motions of sewing – thread the needle, tie off the ends, break the thread in their teeth, etc – but they had no thread, and no needle.

Another gimmick was 'table tennis'. Two men would go

through the motions of playing a fast game of table tennis, in an open area between the huts, or in the road. A crowd of prisoners would gather and all the heads would move together as the 'ball' went from end to end. The Chinese would notice the crowd and inevitably investigate. From behind the crowd it would look very realistic, but as soon as the Chinese tried to push through to see what was going on everyone would turn and move silently away. The Chinese were completely baffled and mystified by these things and probably thought we were all mad. (Not a bad diagnosis really!)

I have even seen two full teams, with attendant crowds of supporters, playing 'football', with no ball. There were one or two tug-of-war matches with no rope, and of course 'invisible dogs'. One or two went to great lengths to make dog leads and collars which really looked like an invisible dog was trotting along with them. They caused much laughter by stopping at the office steps and looking nonchalantly around while the 'dog' obviously did its thing on the steps.

Hole digging was said to be a good send-up in other camps, but the only time I saw it done the instructor ordered the prisoners to dig it out again, so it never gained popularity with us. The idea being to dig a hole quickly, then fill it in quicker as the Chinese approached, making them think something was buried there, so they would dig it out.

Some of my friends formed a band and singing group. They were all musically inclined and came up with the best music we were ever likely to hear in that place. One played drums quite well, using an upturned enamel bowl, and an old tin, with a small brush for one drumstick. One or two played 'paper and comb'. The star player was the bass guitarist, whose guitar consisted of a five gallon oil drum with a cord attached to the handle and stretched to a broom handle, the other end of which was balanced on the rim of the oil drum. By increasing or decreasing the pull on the cord, higher or lower notes could be played. He became quite expert.

A couple of my friends from Cheltenham were good singers, and became quite popular with their harmonized songs. Some men were poetically inclined and could remember poems they had learnt years before. Some wrote their own poems.

At Christmas 1952 the Chinese gave us each a little red notebook, ostensibly to take notes on lectures. On the front it had in English: 'Merry Christmas 1952', and below that a copy of the Commie 'peace dove'. The notebooks came in very handy for copying songs and poems which we then swapped around for reading. As we had nothing to read except Communist propaganda the notebooks became a fund of reading and amusement, good for passing the time.

The air war was above us almost every day. American jet fighters would often plough almost the whole of a clear blue sky with their vapour trails. Great formations of them streaked through the sky, usually at a vast height, but occasionally a few would come down to lower altitudes. Two or three times, low enough to recognise the familiar white star markings. We envied them their war, with their coffee and doughnuts, within the hour. Not even knowing of our boiled water and sorghum.

Aerial combat over the camp usually led to great speculation on all sides as to who had shot down whom. It was all too high up to make a good spectator event. On one occasion a jet fighter crashed a few miles away, the pilot coming down by parachute about a mile from the camp, up the road to the North. The Chinese were jubilant, it had to be an 'Imperialist aggressor'. But when a truck rolled through the camp about half an hour later with a rather battered Oriental gentleman in flying kit sat in it, there was a different tune!

On three occasions the camp attracted the most unwelcome attentions of lone US medium bombers. These raids were at night. Twice we were bombed and once strafed. On the first bombing raid, I think three people were killed, one was a Chinese cook. The other two, strangely enough, were captured US aircrew officers. The second bombing raid didn't touch the camp, but the strafing run with a trigger happy belly-gunner rolling it out with a big .50 calibre came too close for comfort. All he really did was break a lot of roof tiles and scorch one man's back, but what a damn row he made about it! Several rounds hit our hut, but none entered our room. In the next hut a man sat up when he heard the shooting and a bullet scorched down his bare back and drilled a hole where he had been lying. In a camp full of soldiers he must have been the only one who didn't roll on to his stomach at the first shot.

One good story came out of the first bombing raid. A man had just left the latrine when he heard the bombs start to whistle. His soldier's instinct made him turn and dive back through the doorway where he collided with another and they both went in the pit.

During an air alert one night, when the bombers were going over very high up, we were lying in ditches around the camp, just in case. One of my friends had a watch with a bright luminous dial and an instructor shouted at him, 'So and so, put that watch out! Put it out at once!' Except for the panic in his voice I would have thought he was joking. He was deadly serious!

I think it was the same instructor on another air alert occasion, told us to be quiet, and stop talking – as if the aircrews would hear us.

The day after the first bombing raid the Chinese got up a petition for everyone to sign. At least, I presume the Chinese thought it up, – I could be wrong. The petition was to be sent to Kaesong, where the peace negotiations had recently commenced, to complain to the UN and accuse the US Air Force of deliberately bombing defenceless POW's in a registered POW camp.

There was some considerable argument between us and our captors over the extreme wording of the petition, which resulted in them changing the text quite a bit. There was also some considerable discussion between all the prisoners of war as to whether or not we should sign such a thing. At the time there was a lot of speculation about whether or not the free world knew of our existence. In the end most of us signed the petition. At least, we printed our name, rank and number on the sheet of paper, thereby, (hopefully) letting the free world know that, at that date we were alive, and POW's in Communist hands. It would also indicate our exact whereabouts in Korea. As far as most of us could see, the petition had considerably more going for us than for the commies – if it was ever presented in full to the UN negotiators at Kaesong. I never did hear if it reached them.

In the summer of 1952 there was a bacterialogical warfare scare. The Chinese were quite convinced the Americans were dropping some 'dreaded lurgy' on them. They had lots of photographs of the canisters used, some with flies crawling all around them. We were all inoculated against God knows what (tap-water I expect) and a great hygiene campaign ensued. The announcement that the US had started this type of warfare nearly started a massacre in the camp. We were all rushed to the parade ground by the angriest, biggest contingent of guards we ever saw. There were extra machine guns around the parade ground and all the Chinese looked very upset – at us!

The camp commandant started the ball rolling going berserk in Chinese. We wondered what the hell we had done. Speculation ran rife as he ranted on. After a couple of minutes he stopped, there was a silence as the interpreter glared around at everyone to keep up the pressure, then he started: 'The American Capitalist Imperialist Aggressors have commenced to use Black Treacle Warfare!'

A deathly silence lasting two seconds, then a voice from the back of the British contingent shouted 'In barrels or baksheesh*?' The whole camp dissolved into gales of laughter – and of course the Chinese went mad. More guards appeared and rushed up to the ranks of prisoners looking all set to shoot. The camp commandant looked fit to burst. It took a while to sort it all out, but the other interpreters present – the only Chinese who knew what was wrong – managed to get things under control before it became a massacre. A different interpreter took over, and put us in the picture. There were yells of disbelief from the American prisoners, which got the guards on edge again. I was damn glad to get off the parade ground that day. But it was worth it!

A day or two later there was a swarm of big black flies down by the river. An American prisoner was found stuffing them into his mouth as fast as he could. Can't remember what happened to him – whether he went to jail, hospital or neither, but I do remember it upset the Chinese quite a bit. I think he was trying to prove he didn't believe the 'Black Treacle Warfare' story. He may have just been round the bend – mentally deranged.

Another time there was a near riot when we had to organise a 'concert'. There was to be singing, stories, poems, etc. A few things went OK at the start, and the whole camp was on the parade ground as per lectures. Then one of our lot got up on the stage to read what was claimed to be a poem from the 'English classics'. I don't know what he had on the sheet of paper, which had been vetted by the Chinese, but one thing is

---

* Baksheesh – pronounced Bukshee, to spare, loose, extra, left over.

sure – it wasn't the poem he came out with! I can't remember how it went at the start but a few lines – the ones which made the shit hit the fan – I'll never forget.

> They seek him here, they seek him there
> They seek the bastard everywhere
> Will he be shot or will he be hung?
> That damned elusive Mao-Tse-Tung?

The camp went wild, but nothing compared with our captors. The great poet was bounced into jail so fast his feet never touched the ground. The camp was in uproar in his defence. A nasty looking situation was saved by 'Ding', one of our Chinese platoon leaders, whose English was almost nil. As one of the guards rushed up behind us Ding snatched the Tommy gun from him, shouted 'office' (one of the few words he knew in English) and started off in the direction of our huts. We all fell in behind him and went back to our rooms. The 'concert' was over.

The camp jail was a place to be avoided if at all possible. Our food was bad enough for the first eighteen months, but in jail it was much worse – and much less – if that is possible. It wasn't the posh jail all the namby-pambies of today claim to be 'Victorian', overcrowded, cruel, etc. – that would have been heaven to us. No, the jail in that prison camp was rough. It ranged from the cushy, which was standing or sitting in one position day and night for a week or two, with an ever alert guard to make sure you did, to hanging up by your handcuffs from a beam for long periods and, worst of all, I can only imagine the 'boxes'.

The idea of jail in most cases, was to get a confession in writing, with a signature from the 'offender'. Very often the charges were absolutely ridiculous and men just would not sign confessions to rape and murder when all they had tried to do was go home.

The boxes were just that. Boxes. I only saw them once, from the outside, thank goodness. They were about three or four feet square. Some were a bit smaller. Made of wood. The only opening into the box – once you were in there – was a gap at floor level big enough to push a rice bowl through. (Three inches high by six inches wide).

Men were put in those boxes for two or three weeks. In at least one case it was for a month. They were handcuffed with their hands behind their backs. They usually had dysentery, but they never came out of the box or had their handcuffs removed for anything. They ate and drank like a dog. The guards kicked or banged the box often, to keep them awake – so they wouldn't miss too much of it by sleeping. There were variations on treatment in the boxes: some men were brought out once or twice per day to the latrine, some were not handcuffed, some had handcuffs with their hands in front of them. It varied, but it was all rough.

There were also cages. These were used same as the boxes, only the guards could watch you didn't get any sleep.

One man in particular Derek Kinney, who made an absolute fetish of escaping and has since written a book, *The Wooden Boxes*, about his escapades and horrific treatment as a POW in Korea, was given the full treatment at various times throughout his captivity, but never cracked. He was a member of the Royal Northumberland Fusiliers. I had met him after capture and knew him well by sight.

One incident I remember well but don't remember when it was, possibly late 1951 or spring of 1952, he had escaped and been captured again, and we knew he was in solitary confinement. Some of us were sitting on the verandah outside our room when along came Kinney, looking rather roughed up but calmly nonchalant, as usual.

'Hullo Lofty, how's the arm shaping up?' he said.

'OK thanks,' says I. 'I thought you were in solitary again.'

He just grinned, 'I am, but they haven't missed me yet!'

He was so cool about it I thought he was joking.

Sure enough he wasn't joking, but he wasn't ready to make another run for it either, and I believe he got back into solitary before anyone found out. How the hell he did it I don't know. Kinney spent most of his captivity in solitary, sometimes in the boxes or cages, and at least once hanging by his handcuffs being beaten up. But that's another story.

Colonel Carne spent most of his captivity in solitary confinement too. Don't know what the excuse was but I think it was because he would not 'conform'. The political nuts tried to indoctrinate him, and were often attempting to make him admit to being wrong to serve in Korea. Someone who spent some time in the next cell to Colonel Carne told us something which cheered us considerably. One of the political nuts was yelling at Joe, over and over again, 'Have you realised your mistake?'

Joe Carne eventually answered. 'I am an officer in the British Army. I do not make mistakes!'

We didn't hear what the nut made of that one, but I would imagine he completely flipped.

While in captivity Colonel Carne carved a small cross from a lump of rock. After his release, and return to UK, Joe gave the cross to Gloucester Cathedral, where I believe it still is.

Another thorn in the side of Chinese efforts toward peace and quiet was our adjutant, Captain Farrar-Hockley*. He was another escape-o-maniac, but, like young Kinney he only had to see a half chance and he was through it! The problem with that method is you are always on the run in an even weaker state than necessary due to solitary confinement and almost nil rations.

I think the adjutant was the best chance we had of anyone escaping. He could navigate, had some knowledge of the area and where he was starting from, was well switched on mentally and had been physically very fit. Had he played it cool long enough to build up his resources and given himself a fair chance I feel sure he would have cracked it. But, like Kinney he was a marked man from the start and had to escape sometimes from a prison within a prison. Farrar-Hockley's best attempt got him to within sight of the sea on the Korean west coast, and that was the route three of us from Cheltenham were intending to take in the autumn of 1953.

Once I had pinned down our position on the map, and built up a reasonable picture of the geography of North Korea it was, in my case, a matter of waiting for my arm to improve enough. The plot was to move west, keeping to the mountains and more remote areas, moving only at night, hiding by day until we reached the coast, then find a boat and get over the horizon during darkness. The fruit in the mountains and crops in cultivated areas would feed us at that time of year. But it was not to be. Perhaps very luckily for me as, if recaptured and beaten up, etc. I might have lost the use of my arm entirely.

There was not a lot of beating up of prisoners in jail, but it

* *The Edge of the Sword*

was not uncommon. Anyone who escaped from the camp was charged (on their return) with attempting to contact Imperialist agents, attempting to sabotage the Korean war effort, trespassing on the property of the Korean people and a whole catalogue of weird and wonderful intrigues to which they were required to sign a confession.

As an illustration of ridiculous charges, a friend of mine was talking to another prisoner, facing towards a path about 75 yards away, along which a Korean girl came walking. The Chinese guard standing a few yards away rushed up and hauled my friend away to the jail, where they charged him with attempted rape, and for days tried to make him sign a confession. A lot of men said they would have been flattered to have been charged with rape at 75 yards.

Early in 1952 the brainwashing campaign was going full blast. To be able to do a better job the Chinese re-organised the prisoners into racial groups. We were moved nearer the town, into what had been guards quarters, thereby splitting us further from the Americans. All the black Americans were marched off to another camp miles away.

It was when the black prisoners were being sent off that the Chinese came up against the Brit at his best. We had one black gentleman in our ranks. He was a cook, attached to the Glosters, and was from St Helena. Steve, we called him and there was no argument about colour – Steve was black, like, ever so black. In those days there was very little, or no colour prejudice in UK. I had never seen or heard of it, except with the Americans. Somehow we didn't connect our black people with the American 'nigger'.

The Chinese swooped on Steve and were hauling him away to go with the 'niggers'. The Brit contingent raised hell. There were shouts of 'He's a Brit, he belongs with us' and 'He's not a bloody nigger, he's British!' I remember seeing Steve's worried face turn into a big flashing grin when the Chinese hesitated and he saw we were all on his side.

Some of our people got a couple of the interpreters and explained that Steve was British and should stay with the British. Colour or creed had nothing to do with it if you were a Brit! The Chinese were thrown into confusion by all this – and several hundred prisoners there to prove it by yelling, 'We want Steve.' This went against all the Commie patter about racialism

An air photograph of the town of Chongsung, North Korea, parts of which were designated POW Camp No 1 by the communists. From early 1952, British prisoners were housed in the group of buildings closest to the northern (top) POW marker. Chinese guards and administration personnel lived in the double row of light-coloured buildings just south of (below) the British quarters. The camp jail and more guards' accommodation was in the muddle of buildings to the left of the cross marked on the photo. Officers and Sergeants were housed in a separate area somewhere south and east of the town centre, possibly near the southern (bottom) POW marker. American POWs were housed to the north of the British area (off the photo), but not in the buildings at the top edge of the photo, as I believe these were left empty when the British left them in early 1952. Presumably there was another marker north of the American quarters, otherwise their part of the camp would have been outside the 'marked' POW camp area.

Other places mentioned in the text are the camp parade/lecture area, which is at the top of the photo (a rectangular field with the letters POW inked on it) and the 'Japanese Temple'/death house/hospital which cannot be identified for certain but, I believe, is the large dark rectangular building with a courtyard in the middle near the right edge of the photo but level with the jail. Below that can be seen 16 light-coloured huts in four rows of four. These were wooden huts built by the Chinese and housed more guard troops and administration staff; I only saw them just before release.

The photograph was taken on 25 March 1952, from 15,000 feet, by the United States Air Force (*Smithsonian Institute, Washington*).

F86 Sabre of the US Air Force. These were the men we envied high above us in the prison camp, knowing they would soon be back to their coffee and doughnuts. Nevertheless, there was more to it than pretty contrails in the sky. About 70 of them were shot down by the Mig 15s — at a cost of over 700 Mig 15s!! (*Royal Air Force Museum*).

The negative of this photograph was found in the POW camp. We believe it shows the main road through our particular camp, looking north to the US sector from the British sector. POWs are American, in prison winter clothing. Photo probably taken in early 1952, just after the hard winter. 'Boot Hill' was 200 metres to the right (*D.A. Gardiner*).

Above left Two friends in the Glosters' MMG Platoon, with their 'Universal' Carrier at Kimpo a few weeks before the Imjin battle (*Brian Hamblett*).

Above right The same two friends (one in the white shirt, the other with the white T-shirt, jacket open) with other UN POWs, photographed by the Chinese shortly before their release (*Brian Hamblett*).

Below 'Good Ol' Joe' (Lt-Colonel J.P. Carne VC DSO DSC) our popular CO, being chaired to the officers' mess at Kure, Japan, by other recently repatriated Glosters on the day of his release from captivity (*Associated Press*).

Above left A friend, a few weeks after release, on the boat home (*Brian Hamblett*).

Above right 'Sam' Mercer, Glosters, and Rifleman Mitchell, RUR, being greeted by Brigadier Kendrew, Commander of 29 Infantry Brigade at 'Freedom Village' on their release from captivity. They were released in the exchange of sick and wounded POWs in April 1953 (*S. Mercer*).

Below RAF Lyneham, Wilts. My parents and sister meet me off the aircraft in May 1953. (Our uniforms were issued in the size we took before capture.) (*Cheltenham Newspaper Co*).

by the British Imperialists. In the end Steve stayed with us. The camp commandant changed the orders and Steve was classified as a definite Brit, irrespective of colour.

The 'Steve incident' was one of those occasions when Chinese good commonsense overcame Communist indoctrination, and the POW camp authorities, notably the camp commandant, used his head. These occasions were not as few as might be expected. They did Communism no good in our eyes as, without the stupidities of Communism, most of the situations would never have arisen, but they did reinforce a belief, held by many of us, that the Chinese character would eventually triumph over the harsh regime in China.

Quite early on in our days at the prison camp, it was decided, by the Chinese, that flies were a menace to hygiene and we should do something about it. To solve the problem each man was given a 'fly quota'. It started off at twenty flies per day, which had to be produced (dead of course) to be counted by the Chinese Staff. The quota went up after a week or two, to thirty flies per day per man. After a while it became very difficult to fill the quota as flies became somewhat scarce. A simple enough solution to a vast problem. In spite of the original ridicule poured upon the idea by many of us, it worked. Flies went from a big hygiene problem to being practically non existent in about a month or six weeks. None of us minded killing flies, it was the tedious job of collecting and counting which we didn't like. I often wondered about the Chinese platoon leaders who had to count up to one hundred men's fly quotas. Three thousand bloody flies to count every day. That's taking dedication to the limit! It is worth noting the guards and camp administration staff also had 'fly quotas' to fill at that time.

From the day we arrived at the camp all drinking water was boiled. This was done in a big steel tub in the cookhouse, the same tub our sorghum or rice was cooked in. It was a sensible defence against the spread of disease and was one of the first instructions the Chinese gave on our arrival.

The British 'cooks' would boil a tub of water about three or four times every day. When the 'pot' was boiled one of them would shout, 'Hot water up!' and there was usually a mad dash for the cookhouse. Dozens of thirsty prisoners carrying our cans or bowls to be filled. There was always a madder dash when the food was ready, until we were issued with a couple of larger bowls to each squad, in which the squads rations were brought back to the room for equal distribution. The signal that the food was ready was always a call of 'Come and get it!'

All water in the camp came from wells around the streets, which had been the source of water for the townsfolk before we arrived. The well in my part of the camp was about thirty feet deep, and the task of lifting the water was helped by the use of a long pole which had the rope and well bucket attached to one end and a large section of concrete lashed to the other. It worked on the same principle as that employed by the barriers seen at factory entrances and the like, where a large barrier can easily be lifted by one person. Except that in the well's case the pole was upright when left alone and the bucket was lowered by pulling down on the rope.

One of our guards was nicknamed 'Goggles' as he always appeared on duty wearing a pair of fur-lined goggles. He was extra vigilant, screamed abuse and made a damn nuisance of himself at every opportunity. He carried a rifle, with bayonet always fixed, and was very handy at making stabbing motions around anyone on the way to the latrines at night.

Goggles was out in the hills one day as part of the screen around a wood detail. A tree had fallen against some power lines and Goggles, seeing something out of the ordinary, had to use his bayonet as usual. He charged the tree and stuck the bayonet in it. I didn't see it happen, but those who did, reckon Goggles went about twenty metres down the hill in a shower of sparks. A couple of lads from the RUR went and picked him up, recovered the rifle and bayonet, and took him down to a stream, where they commenced to clean him up and try to revive him. He was out cold for a bit, but came round eventually.

Other guards had seen this all happen from a distance, and rushed to their comrade's aid. They brought him back to the guards quarters, where he recovered enough to return to duty within a week or so.

The two prisoners who had shown compassion to another human being were highly praised by the Chinese, much to their embarrassment, and held up as an example to us all. Goggles probably had some brain damage, I don't know. After a few weeks on duty he had to be taken off guard duties. It was quite usual to see his unattended rifle (minus bayonet) leaning against the wall of a hut, while Goggles was inside playing cards with the boys. The Brits were his friends, and from now on could do no wrong.

After the Americans and Brits were completely separated by distance and more sentries, we saw very little of them. Poncho came up one night to bring me a re-supply of weed. (Risking his neck in the process!) Most of our friends in the American camp we now saw only at a distance, at lectures on the parade ground, when we were under close supervision.

To a certain extent I missed the Americans. Some of the hardened old soldiers were good to listen to. Not only their quaint turn of speech – even for Americans – but they were always well up on shit-house rumours. If the war wasn't going to end next week, we were going to be liberated the week after, etc. Few of the Brits believed any of these rumours, and I doubt the Americans were really fooling themselves, but it gave a good flavour to conversation. The only subject worthy of serious discussion was how soon we would get out of there.

Some of the older Americans had seen action in the Pacific, North-West Europe or Italy, and those men were much harder than most others from their country. They were good to talk to, even if only to offset the low morale and degradation of many other Americans. As mentioned earlier the Americans had their 'Three whole days and no candy disease'. From what I saw there were probably hundreds died of just that.

At the other end of the scale there was a very young American who had fooled the Army – or Marines, I can't remember which – into thinking he was two years older than he was. When captured, he had both legs trapped under a knocked out tank, and had both legs sawn off at the knee, without anaesthetic. He had been keen on boxing as a kid and we often saw him being carried by a friend and sparring with others. His morale was always sky high when I saw him. They told us he was still only sixteen years old when he was captured.

One of the real old sweats I knew pretty well, came from the American 'Deep South', his Southern drawl had to be heard to be believed. His remarks about those of his countrymen who, as he put it, 'Couldn't get on their back legs to piss with the wind', were very much to the point. But he was the world's greatest optimist; the least thing in the real news – that given out by the Chinese, as opposed to the latrines – he could turn into another good reason we'd be out and home very shortly.

When General Mark Clark was made commander of UN Forces in Korea, the old sweat claimed he knew the General when he was just a 'Kiddy Cap'n'. He also claimed Mark Clark would have us liberated within a month. 'Lefty,' he said, 'that man is my kind of soldier! When he says shit – you squat, and ask what colour.'

The US Army could have done with more men like that, and less like the one I saw charge a very ill fellow American twenty dollars to fetch a rusty can of muddy water from the river, twenty yards away.

During the last few months of my captivity one or two of our people managed to get work in one of the Chinese offices, doing typing and helping with translation etc. Most of us considered the situation decidedly suspicious so those involved were on very dicey ground. After a while the odd snippet of news from the outside world filtered into the camp and we found there was a radio in the Chinese office which, on the very rare occasions when they were left unguarded our people tuned into the BBC Overseas Service. Hence the reason for the typing etc.

It must have been very difficult to get any news though, as the occasions of being left unguarded must have rarely coincided with a news bulletin. Nevertheless it was by this means that we first heard of the death of King George VI, several weeks after the event. The Chinese had not told us His Majesty had died because we were working class people who would obviously have no interest in the relics of capitalist society – and in any case it may have disrupted our concentration on our political studies. An interesting combination of observations.

Any time we got the chance we would 'send up' our Chinese political instructors. A few well chosen words in the right place could often send them scurrying off to check the details with their books, or higher authority. Some of our people were quite good at it but the only time I remember getting them worried for a few minutes, it was more by accident than deliberate.

At that time the French were not doing so good with their Indo-China problem and we were forever being told of the great achievements of the 'Viet Nam People's Army'. So a few of us from Cheltenham decided we must be the 'Chelt Nam

People's Army', and I mentioned this mythical military formation within earshot of one of the Chinese instructors. He questioned me quite seriously about my connections with this undoubtedly great army, and I told him some of us were in it because that's where we came from, Chelt Nam.

It could have been a good send-up but another instructor became involved about half an hour later and he had obviously made a closer study of the Brit character, done his homework or whatever. The two instructors came to me and the more fluent English speaking new face on the scene said, 'Now, who has been mispronouncing the name of a town in Gloucestershire? You or my friend here?'

There were two main methods for the British prisoners to show dissent in the camp. When there was some problem and we were en masse, someone would start singing 'Land of Hope and Glory'. We found this really wound up the Chinese as they recognised it as a real Imperialist hymn. We often sang it when marching to or from the lectures. It can be very morale lifting, when the opposition think they have scored a point, to hear three or four hundred voices singing a song like that.

The other method was, as far as I know, home grown in the camp. Little hangman's nooses would appear as if by magic in all sorts of places. On the notice board. Over the doorway to the Chinese Office. At each end of the office verandah, right under the noses of the guards. One of the sentries nearly went off his head when he saw a noose hanging from a tree opposite his sentry box. But he looked even more shaken when he returned to his sentry box and found one hanging over the doorway.

In the very savage winter of 1951-52, the cold was the worst I have ever encountered. While washing the 'cans' in hot water the splashes would freeze on the backs of our hands. I know at least one sentry froze to death in his sentry box. Rumour had it there were seven or eight froze to death at their posts that night.

Thanks to the Chinese we were well equipped to withstand the cold. The food had marginally improved by the time winter came, but the greatest life saver was the clothing with which we were issued. One or two rough cotton shirts to supplement our old army shirts, and a suit, hat, gloves and boots made of kapok. Quilted clothes similar to that worn by the Chinese, but not so well made, and blue instead of mustard colour.

We had by then been given a rush or bamboo mat for the floor

of the room, and before the real cold came, we were issued with
two or three heavy quilted eiderdowns which covered the whole
squad at night. The heated floors of the huts did the rest.
Without the issue of those things the Chinese would have had
very few prisoners by the end of that winter.

I think it was in the late autumn of 1952, a very sorry looking
little group of bedraggled prisoners appeared on the road
through the camp. There were about ten or fifteen of them.
Their clothes were in tatters, some were barefoot. They had
North Korean Army guards. In spite of the heavy threatening
attitude of their guards, some of our people found there were a
couple of Brits among them, and immediately rushed to the
Chinese to request they do something about these poor
scarecrows passing through.

The Chinese stopped the group, and there began a long
parley with the Korean guards. Eventually the prisoners were
handed over to the Chinese. I have a feeling the Koreans were
glad to be rid of them.

One of the 'new' prisoners came to my squad, which had
been reduced to eight or nine on the last re-shuffle. They had
had a pretty rough time as prisoners of the North Koreans,
and, I believe had been more or less on the move ever since
capture. The man who came to my squad was a Marine
Commando whose small boat had been blown onto the enemy
shore by a sudden storm after the engine failed. He was
actually captured in his swimming trunks, which he was still
wearing when I first saw him, several months after capture. He
also had a piece of tatty blanket draped round his shoulders.
Not the best gear with which to face a North Korean winter.

Conditions generally improved steadily throughout our
captivity. By the end of 1951 we were getting steamed bread
perhaps once every two or three weeks. This replaced the
evening meal of sorghum. We were also getting a bowl of
sloppy sorghum in the morning for breakfast. In mid 1951, a
week or two after arriving at the camp, we had been issued
with a rice bowl and spoon each. By late summer the 'greens'
were alternated occasionally with bean sprouts (young shoots
from soya beans) and later by actual beans. At first there was
more water than beans, but gradually the ration increased.

In late Autumn 1951, maybe early winter, we had 'pork'. For
one meal only. One average size pig was killed, chopped up and

boiled in a lot of water to feed about five hundred men. Anyone who got more than one tiny bit of meat was lucky. Nevertheless, the water tasted bloody marvellous.

At Christmas the Chinese put on extra rations, we had 'pork' again, at about the same ratio as before, and chicken as well. I think we had chicken before Xmas 1951, once or twice. Six or seven chickens, plucked, chopped up small (bones and all) and boiled in a lot of water to feed about five hundred men. Again the water was heavenly. Rotten fish appeared once or twice, but even we starved critters had problems with that.

Gradually, through 1952, the food improved. Pork and chicken came more often, and more of it. Steamed bread became a weekly event by late 1952. Sorghum began to be replaced by rice. Millet disappeared altogether. Greens were occasional, having been replaced by soya beans by late 1952.

Sometime in late 1952, perhaps at Christmas, we were each issued with a toothbrush, toothpaste, soap and towel. These items were very welcome and raised morale as well as our general hygiene standard.

On two or three occasions, maybe Christmas 1951, May Day 1952 and Christmas 1952, our captors surprised us by issuing every man with a good tot of wine. They called it 'Peace Wine'. It amounted to somewhere between one and two tots, as per spirits, and was just about raw alcohol. One or two people still had their petrol fuelled cigarette lighters, and found they went well on 'peace wine', so it was strong all right. Had we been given about five tots each there wouldn't have been much peace in that area. Some of us called it 'firewater'.

By early 1953 we were being fed pretty well by previous standards. No one should get the idea we were being fattened up though, because although by the time of my release I had been on comparatively marvellous rations for two or three months, I was considerably underweight, only nine stone ten pounds (136 lbs). Normal food was hard going when I was first released, but in two days I put on 8lbs.

Reports in Commie newspapers in the United Kingdom and elsewhere, played up the pork and chicken we received so that their readers were very likely given the impression we were living the life of Riley. At least two Commies came to Korea to see for themselves. One was a Brit, a woman; the other, a male, was Australian. The Aussie brought us a real football and was told what to do with it – inflated! By that time the Chinese had already produced a couple of footballs for us and gave us a certain amount of freedom to play matches on the big parade ground. So, telling the traitor Commie what to do with his ball was no problem.

The fact that Commies from back home could come and wander around in North Korea while British troops were fighting and dying with the Commonwealth Division to the south, struck us as significant. It meant there was no difference between our Commies and the rest of them, anywhere in the world.

In our minds British Commies took on a different aspect. They obviously condoned stabbing Poland in the back, the slaughter of the Polish Officer Corps at Katyn Wood, the 'Siberian Salt Mines' for political dissenters, the wholesale slaughter of all who would not conform to the ideals of Lenin, Marx and Co. More to the point they condoned North Korea's invasion of South Korea in 1950, and the ensuing slaughter, which swept Korea from end to end.

We did not hate the Chinese. They were people like us, who were trying to do their job the best they could. They were fighting for their country and were respected for it. But almost every British prisoner hated the system which had caused the war by trying to force itself on other people. We respected the Chinese much as we had respected the German troops during World War Two, but Communism was hated equally with Fascism.

Dictatorship by one man, or dictatorship by one party, what's the difference? Both become a law unto themselves, trampling on the laws of their own country, - before starting on someone else's. The methods become irrelevant so long as the end result is achieved. Total subjugation of the masses.

The traitors from UK who came snivelling around in Korea should have been accorded the same treatment they would have received had it been the other way round.

Can you imagine the welcome home party if a Chinese journalist or politician had hobnobbed with the Americans in South Korea? Talked to Chinese prisoners of war, told them they had been liberated from a dictatorship, then gone home to tell how well treated they were. Do you think there would have been a newspaper in Peking which would have dared employ such a person – let alone publish anything they wrote? These British Commies do not think past their noses to see they are only free to hobnob with the enemy because their home is in a democracy. Their attitude is to say 'Capitalism' is too weak to oppose them – as they represent the people.

We may not have a salt mine patch to send them to, but we do have a little place called Rockall. If they are not bothered about the means – the end result is the same.

CHAPTER NINE

Repatriation

In March 1953, having been called to the office, I was surprised to be given a thorough medical examination by a Chinese doctor. He spent a lot of time examining my arm and shoulder, making notes on a pad every few minutes. The examination lasted about half an hour, after which I was told to return to my room, – without explanation.

Medical facilities at the camp had improved somewhat over the time we had been there. At first there was nothing. Then, several weeks after we arrived, a Chinese woman doctor appeared. She could speak fairly good English, had studied at Edinburgh. She was really a surgeon but could do very little for us as she had little or no surgical equipment. Her only medicine as far as I know was iodine. It was used for everything – even toothache. I don't remember when she left, or what the medical situation was for the last few months. Men still died occasionally in the American camp, but the burial party was a comparative rarity on Boot Hill.

In mid-April 1953 I was again called to the office. This time they told me to report back in one hour with my kit as I would be going into hospital. There was a mad rush around the camp to say goodbye to my friends, some of whom gave me their home addresses on a tobacco packet. Rumour had been rife that there was going to be an exchange of disabled prisoners so we were not completely taken by surprise as everyone seemed to think I would be a prime candidate. I personally thought that in my case it was more likely the Chinese would give me the treatment required to cross me off the 'disabled list', if they qualified me for anything at all. The Chinese told me nothing, except where to go and what to do.

Arriving at the hospital, the same old Japanese temple on the hill, where so many had died, when it was just a 'death house', I found it was now a real hospital with proper beds, real nurses, doctors, the whole works. An English speaking Chinese officer told me they would operate that night to remove a bullet from my ribs. A feeling of doubt crept into my mind but the familiar feel of a clean, efficient hospital was reassuring. Late in the evening a Chinese who, later, turned out to be the surgeon came to examine my arm and ribs. He seemed efficient, had the confident air of a man who knew what he was doing. I felt further reassured. About midnight, a nurse came and escorted me to a small operating theatre. All the usual preparations were made, a nurse told me the operation would be completed with only a local anaesthetic. For some reason I felt relieved they were not going to put me out.

All went well until the surgeon obviously found the bullet was jammed into bone, and he had to get some bigger tools to cope. That's when the air raid siren sounded and all the lights went out. About two seconds later two of the nurses had hand torches going, – as if they had expected the air raid. The surgeon worked on steadily, while the bombers droned overhead, and his patient sweated blood – thinking what a stupid situation to be caught in if those bombers decided to unload.

Listening to that menacing rumble and roar in the sky above, waiting for the first whistle of the bombs, deciding which way to roll off the operating table must have passed the time quickly. Before I knew it the surgeon had stitched up the wound, handing me a very battered tracer bullet and looking pleased with his handiwork.

I hardly realised I'd been holding one of the nurses' hands until I reached for the bullet and she was laughing and rubbing her crushed fingers.

One of the nurses said, 'OK go back to your bed. We will look at it again in the morning.' The bombers were distant, and soon after I reached my bed the 'All Clear' sounded.

Early in the morning the surgeon and a few other Chinese doctors and nurses came to check the site of the operation. They seemed well satisfied and left. Half an hour later I was cleaning my teeth in the yard when a nurse called me and told me to go at once to the gate at the main entrance. My first thought was to put away my washing kit, but the nurse stopped me and said, 'I will take that. You must go to the gate – at once.'

At the gate a Chinese officer checked my name off a list and told me to go out of the gate to sit with some other prisoners on the steep hillside in front of the Temple Hospital. There were several other prisoners, British and American, already sitting on the grass, no one knew what was going on. A few more men came out to join us until after five or ten minutes there were about twenty or thirty of us sitting on the hillside, which was stepped at about two foot intervals.

A Chinese officer walked to a position below and in front of us. He looked us all over carefully, spoke briefly to other Chinese hovering nearby then smiled and addressed the assembled prisoners. 'Gentlemen, there has been an agreement to exchange sick and wounded prisoners. You are going home.'

There then started a dream-like, confused, hazy few days which I would like to remember more clearly. Some of it, that is. First of all, I didn't feel excited, being convinced it was all just another dream. The whistles would blow any minute, awakening me to another dawn, another roll call, another lecture, probably sorghum and beans. In any case, after all the months of haggling and mind changing at the peace negotiations it was just as likely they would all fall out and cancel the lot by lunchtime.

We were not allowed back into the hospital. Our kit was brought to us in the wooden huts we were taken to. There were some speeches by the Chinese, they were short and all except the first – from the camp commandant – were in English. There was a complete lack of propaganda patter, the main theme of the speeches being to wish us and our families health and happiness in the future. It was one of the few times our captors spoke to us with complete sincerity. I am quite sure those Chinese who spoke to us were happy for us to be going home.

We were given a quick meal with strong Chinese wine to wash it down, taken out to open trucks, loaded, checked and away we went. The little convoy of three or four trucks rumbled northwards through the prison camp, but I was too disbelieving, too full up at having to leave all my friends – who stood at the roadside – to do more than wave weakly as we passed them.

Once clear of the camp we gathered speed and made good time, along a winding road through wooded mountains, to a prison camp at, I believe, Pyoktong, close to the Yalu River. More trucks loaded with prisoners joined us and after an hour or two we were on the road again, with a much bigger convoy heading south and west until night.

At night we stopped somewhere, I've no idea where. Memories of that journey are dominated by pain. Where we stopped or even how many days we travelled is all lost in a haze of pain. Strong red wine helped deaden the pain but it deadened the memory as well. The roads were dirt roads, a bit the worse for wear and showing plenty of signs of the continual bombing. They were full of holes and humps, and the trucks went like hell. Every morning I bust my stitches and bled all over the place. Every night they stitched me up again, without anaesthetic. The operation wound and the bleeding didn't bother me much but the continual bouncing and jolting played hell with my shoulder and arm. There were no seats in the truck. At times we were all in a heap on the floor, trying to find something to hang on to. Obviously there was a deadline to meet, as some of the Chinese were concerned for our well being, but said we had to move quickly.

At last we came to a place with a bigger building than usual, full of bunk beds. We got ourselves cleaned up. My blood-soaked clothes were replaced. We were thoroughly searched from head to toe. All our kit was searched and I noticed with horror that the tobacco packet with my friends home addresses on it was now a tobacco packet with part of an escape map on it. I had checked my kit at the hospital – and destroyed the wrong tobacco packet!

The Chinese searching my kit looked at the rough map, glanced up at me then put it with the rest of my gear. I died a thousand deaths while he finished the search, then he waved me on to join the others.

The moment of release came. My name was called in the last batch of prisoners. It all felt like a dream with the hated whistle just one breath away. Wondering if it was all a trick which would finish up in some horrific punishment cell for having that map. I think we travelled by bus to the exchange point, then were checked again, and walked over to a British ambulance where the familiar uniforms and well fed looking Brits helped us in. The doors banged shut then off we went.

As the ambulance moved steadily along a dirt road, across an open, grassy area I noticed through the window to the left a hill, with three or four plumes of smoke rising near the top. With some shock I realised the plumes of white smoke were made by exploding phosphorous shells. To the right of the road, as we were climbing a slight incline, there were a lot of Chinese troops, moving forward on their stomachs, almost flat in the long grass.

We went over the top of the rise and about one hundred metres down the other side met a platoon of US infantry, walking nonchalantly up the side of the road in single file with their weapons slung on their shoulders. At that particular moment I definitely did not feel 'out of the woods'. The two or three British officers in the ambulance didn't seem at all bothered by the situation outside. It worried me a lot, but I said nothing.

The ambulance ride was a short one, perhaps ten or fifteen minutes before we arrived at 'Freedom Village', a set-up specially prepared to receive repatriated prisoners of war. A very pretty young lady in the uniform of the British Red Cross met me from the ambulance and took me to a large room or tent where there was a very long bar with several barmen standing behind it, all looking eager to serve up a vast array of drinks. There were perhaps half a dozen people in the room. None of them were ex-POW's.

One of the barmen said, 'What would you like Name any drink you fancy.' The Red Cross girl said, 'They claim they can serve any drink in the world at this place. Go on, try them.'

The whistle must surely blow now. I said, 'Banana milk shake, please,' and it likely took all of three or four seconds for a huge banana milk shake to land in front of me.

I remember looking at it in amazement. Several people were laughing, I may have been one of them.

I don't remember seeing any other ex-prisoners at Freedom Village. I had been released with a batch of mostly Americans, also, somewhere along the way my dressing had been changed, the site of the recent operation had been checked by a British medical officer, who had nodded his approval at the work of the Chinese surgeon. I had also been weighed and was rather surprised to find I only weighed 9 stone 10 pounds (61.7 kg). I didn't feel that skinny. Before capture I had been roughly 15 stone 8 lbs (98.4 kg) By the time I arrived at the bar the others had, I believe, been flown out by helicopter.

The Red Cross girl sat with me while I sipped that marvellous milk shake. She asked my name and unit, then for the address of my next of kin. Afterwards keeping up a quiet, lighthearted patter, which was great, all about the bar and Freedom Village. I didn't feel so alone and out of touch.

After about ten minutes the military machine took over and took me to a room where I answered a lot of questions, then to another room where I got rid of my prison uniform and put on a British combat suit for the first time.

The Red Cross girl did her job well. My parents were glad to hear I had been released but very worried that I had been released in an exchange of wounded prisoners. They had hardly time to get worried before receiving a telegram from the Red Cross girl telling them she had seen me and I was O.K. She will never know how much we appreciated that telegram.

Somewhere along the way we were told 22 British prisoners, considered to be unfit for further military service, had been exchanged for over 700 Chinese prisoners. Someone said, 'Now you can work out what you are worth in Chinese.'

I asked when they thought the rest of the prisoners would be released. 'Not until the war is over.' My thoughts kept going back to the camp, the friends I had left behind. Anyway, that bloody whistle would end all this baloney in a minute. The prison camp was easier to believe than all I was now confronted with. It got worse.

I was the last British ex-prisoner to be moved from 'Freedom Village' to hospital. The whole United Nations press had waited days – or perhaps weeks – to get an interview with us at Freedom Village. A British officer put me in the picture about the press. He said all the other British ex-prisoners had refused a press interview and were now gone. I was the last hope as there would be no press interviews in hospital. The decision was mine entirely. Knowing nothing of press interviews or the world of international news, contact with the press at that time was pretty low on my list of priorities. I didn't relish the thought but for some stupid reason I thought of the problems of the press and said OK, I would do it.

Two British Intelligence officers briefed me on how to cope. They reminded me – as if I needed reminding – there were still a lot of men in Communist hands so be careful what I said. We agreed between us that any questions which shouldn't be answered they would tap my leg under the table, all I had to do was wait for the next question. They would sit either side of me and fend off the more stupid questions openly.

We went into the press interview room to be immediately blinded by scores of flash-bulbs. There were a hell of a lot of people there, all banked up like in a sports stadium. I kept the answers short, saying as little as possible. Someone came forward and tossed an address card onto the table in front of me. It had on it, in the form of an address, 'J.V. Stalin. Done in Proper, By Malenkov.' (Still have that card, that's how I remember the words.)

I don't know what my reactions were supposed to mean, but I sensed a lot of people were interested. Then the questions started again. After a few minutes the Intelligence people got me out of there. The next thing I remember is shaking hands with the Red Cross girl then getting into a helicopter. The 'chopper' took me to a military hospital in Seoul, where I got another shower, my dressing changed and a clean soft bed.

There was food, but don't remember what it was, or even where I had my first 'good' food for two years. After all those months of longing for 'real' food, when I got it I couldn't eat it. A few bites of anything and I felt full up – fit to bust.

We were in an American military hospital. In the same ward there were American ex-prisoners who had been released that day. The last thing I remember hearing before sleep crept over me was a whining American voice from the other side of the ward telling a crowd of people how he had seen hundreds of American prisoners driven over a cliff to their deaths, by the Chinese, or North Koreans.

I remember thinking: 'This is where the bullshit begins – if that whistle don't blow.' It was 21 April 1953.

The next morning no whistle, but we arose early, got cleaned up, went to an airfield and boarded a 'Dakota'. I don't remember how long the flight was. It was great to be really covering some miles without a great increase in pain. The pain in my shoulder and hand was still like a big toothache, but with my great faith in medical science I thought our surgeons would cure it with a few deft cuts in the right places. I can't say I was looking forward to the waiting time. In fact, I expected they would operate in Japan.

We landed somewhere in Japan and were taken at once to

the British Commonwealth Military Hospital at Kure. Once there we came under Commonwealth control completely. I began to really take on the feeling of really being free. The hospital staff were very efficient and very human, not always an easy combination. Commonwealth set-ups always struck me that way, a sort of easy-going super efficiency. Men who served with the 1st Commonwealth division in Korea said that feeling went right through the division. At soldier level it gives a great feeling of confidence. It has been said that 1st Commonwealth Division was one of the best divisions ever put in the field, anywhere. Its record shows that is probably true.

Just before my release, I met a young soldier, Pete, who had been captured only six months previously. He was in the Welch Regiment, and had been blinded when captured. His home was not far from mine, in the Cotswolds. Pete was full of how good the Commonwealth Division was. He made me feel I had missed out by not having been part of it. Other people we met gave the same impression. I had never known pride in a division before.

In Kure, we were all given a thorough going over by the Army doctors. I soon realised there was not going to be a quick solution to my crippled arm. The best advice they could give was carry on as before. It seems they thought I had done a damn good job so far. A specialist who examined me said if I'd had the same injuries in England and gone straight into hospital, my chances of living would only have been 50-50. The fact that I had not only survived under adverse conditions but had managed to recover a good deal of movement in the arm surprised them.

The X-rays they took showed I was still carrying eighteen pieces of shrapnel in my chest, arms and back, but no sign of the other bullet. (There was a note on my medical records, 'Query plastic bullet?) It has never turned up.

The shrapnel was not worth digging out. That was easy to accept as, without X-rays, I would never have known it was there. Some had come out in boils during captivity. A little has come out since. The hardest thing to accept was the thought of being crippled. The arm was so weak, thin and almost useless. I had thought an operation or two would fix it. I was assured that good food and time, plus continual exercising would very likely give me a reasonable arm, eventually. One of the doctors made my two years' imprisonment seem worthwhile when he said the arm would almost certainly have been amputated if I had not been captured.

It was obvious that food would soon make a difference somewhere as only two or three days after release I had put on 8 pounds, being ten stone four pounds when weighed in Japan.

By the time we had been in Kure a day or two it was beginning to sink in that we had not done so bad at the Imjin River after all. The Glosters were now famous for holding out long enough to delay the main Chinese offensive at that time. By stopping them from using the road – to move their guns and supplies south – for an extra day or two, gave the UN time to form a stop line which crumbled the whole Chinese spearhead, and our people were back on the Imjin within a month. Nevertheless, the feeling of failure, which had hung over me for two years, persisted.

Later, much later, I learned that 29 Brigade, on 22 April 1951, had six Chinese Divisions, about 54,000 men, all to themselves. In fact, because of the importance of the road through our area the Glosters were elected for the main thrust of the Chinese attack, and were hit first by three divisions of the Chinese 63rd Army (27,000 men) with elements of the 64th Army to our west. The 63rd Army is estimated to have suffered over 11,000 casualties by the morning of 25 April 1951 and was replaced by the 65th Army whose job was to finish off the Glosters then advance south as fast as possible. It is worth noting the Glosters, thanks to heavy reinforcements, were operational again within a couple of weeks, whereas the Chinese 63rd Army was withdrawn back to China and did not take further action in the Korean war.

The feeling of being a failure diminished. The resentment of those clowns who sent us into action with out-dated weapons against those sort of odds – well, enough said.

We were not allowed to leave the hospital while in Kure, so the nurses volunteered to do any shopping for us. I asked my nurse to get me a good camera, so I could take photos on the way home. She got me a very good cmaera and several rolls of film which I used up rapidly over the next week.

After about three days at Kure, we boarded a Royal Air Force Hastings for our flight back to UK. On doctor's orders our limit was eight hours flying per day. This meant it would take a week at least to get home.

Our first stop was at Clarke Field, a US Air Force Base near Manila, in the Philippines. At Clarke Field, I insisted on having a tooth out. It gave me a dog's life every time we got airborne, so out it came. At least that was a pain which I could do something about.

The Hastings we were in was adapted for casualty evacuation. We had four or five stretcher cases aboard, two or three of which were men who had recently been wounded and not ex-prisoners. There was plenty of room in the aircraft, as it was not even half full. Next stop was Singapore, where we again spent the night in hospital, then on to Colombo, Ceylon, the next morning. I remember nearly making myself sick on fresh pine-apple in the hospital at Colombo. From Ceylon to India, then on to Habaniya (I think) in Iraq (I think) where the Air Force base was very proud of its beautiful gardens, in the middle of a desert.

Our last night's stop was in Malta, where we each received a welcome home letter from Lady Mountbatten and an apology for not being there to greet us, as she had to leave the island just before we arrived. All the way home the forces did a great job of keeping the press, etc. away from us. We were really well looked after. There were many doctors, nurses, orderlies, cooks, whose day to day work touched our lives at that 'edgy' time, who will never know how just being normal and doing their job helped tremendously with a difficult adjustment in our minds. Little did they know I was now awaiting that whistle with ever increasing dread and daily increasing certainty that it would blow any minute. I don't know if any of the others had the same things in their minds. I was afraid to mention it for fear of looking stupid – or giving some clown the idea of blowing a whistle.

Eventually the green fields of England were below us, one of the best sights I have ever seen in my life. We landed at RAF Lyneham, in Wiltshire, where my parents and sister were wait-ing to meet me off the aircraft.

We are not an emotional family, so it was just a matter of 'Hi, Maw, hi, Paw, hi Jan' and I was home. It was great to see them there, happy faces and words of welcome. Mother's obvious relief that I wasn't crippled: 'They'll fix all that in a week or two'. The little sister I had left behind nearly three years before had grown a foot or so, and now looked almost grown-up. I didn't recognise her at first.

Half an hour later we went our separate ways. They went

home and I went, with the others, to the RAF hospital at
Wroughton near Swindon, for the night. The next day we were
taken by ambulance to the Army Hospital at Tidworth, on
Salisbury Plain, to get our final check-up and documentation
before going on leave. I think we spent the night at Tidworth,
then (each with a nurse as escort) we were sent home.

Those of us going to Cheltenham area, about four or five,
went by train from Swindon. I remember looking from the
train when we were on an embankment and for the first time
seeing a mass of television aerials. I asked someone what they
were and we all stared in amazement at these strange shapes
sprouting up from all the houses. The nurses thought this was
hilarious and we all finished up getting probably the best laugh
we've ever got from television.

At Cheltenham Station we had a problem. The nurses were
all going home for the week-end once they had delivered us to
our families, but as we all were catching taxis home from the
station, this seemed to be taking duty too far. Except in the case
of Pete, who, being blind we allowed had a problem. He didn't
see it that way, however, and insisted there was no need for his
nurse to ride out to the 'sticks' and back when he and a
taxi-driver could do the job just as well.

The problem was solved when Pete somehow sneaked into a
taxi and went past us shouting 'goodbye' and 'tally-ho'. The way
he took off there was no way we were giving chase, so we said
'many thanks, and cheerio' to the nurses and followed Pete's
example.

So, I arrived home. The walk up the garden path, Mother's
cooking, strong home-made wine – the whole scene of being
really home.

Ann was there, just as I remembered her, to make the
homecoming complete. The physical move from prison camp
to home had taken less than three weeks. The mental move
took longer. Every morning for a week or more I awoke in a
cold sweat – thinking it was that bloody whistle that awoke me.

The taxi-driver who took me home wouldn't take any money
from me, said it was worth every penny to see me get there. A
twelve mile taxi ride for nothing. How did he know? I had sat in
the back and hardly said a word all the way, just gave him
directions.

I soon found out. My picture was in all the local newspapers and probably some of the national ones as well. My stupid grin was all over the cinema newsreels, and on television.

There were 900 British prisoners in Communist hands when we were released, and we 22 were supposed to be the worst cases. 'Unfit for further military service.' So we were news.

For several weeks I found it difficult to pay for anything. Cinemas, buses, taxis, pubs, they all recognised me and refused payment. Everyone wanted to buy me a drink, but I couldn't take it. Half a pint was over my limit. Any more and it wouldn't have stayed down. I tried a few times – not that I was fond of beer anyway, just to be sociable – and suffered for it. I never went in a pub willingly, always press-ganged by a well meaning crowd. People I'd never seen in my life before.

I felt I was stealing human kindness, more deserved by others still rotting in those prison camps, so I shunned the towns. Stayed at home. Mostly just walked and ran through the woods. Went shooting on my own, or sometimes with my father, when he had time. Walked miles through the woods and along country lanes with Ann, when she could be there. Her sense of humour and lighthearted view of life in general did much to restore normality.

After a couple of weeks a letter came from a branch of the Intelligence Service, saying they 'would like to have a chat'. They offered me the choice of going to London or an officer coming to my home. When the officer came he was well pleased at the chance to 'get out of town' and appreciated my reasons too. I told him where I thought my prison camp was. His maps confirmed my position fixes, much to my satisfaction. Then he showed me good air photos of the camp and I was able to fill in a lot of detail about what was which.

He visited my home several days for a couple or three hours at a time. On one occasion I asked his advice about letters I had received from people whose relatives were still classified as 'missing'. Most I had never heard of, but a few I had seen and heard dying. There was no way I could do anything, I couldn't tell people a load of rubbish – neither could I tell them the truth. Some of the memories were too fresh to even try to think of – or connect to real living people. When people came to the house my parents told them I was 'away'.

The officer took note of the men I knew were dead, with certainty. But there were no official guidelines as to how to cope with the problem. He said I'd have to rely on common sense, which had done OK so far. During our conversations it became clear to me that the UN Command had kept quite close tabs on the prison camps and what happened in them. If only we had known of their interest during that two years of captivity, the effect on morale would have been terrific. One tends to feel very much cut off from the outside world when doing the prisoner of war thing, and without the slightest indication that your own military are interested it feels like they don't want to know. I think I mentioned to the Intelligence officer at the time, it would do an absolute power of good if one of the seemingly hundreds of jet fighters forever over our camp could drop down for a quick circle around at low altitude or, better still, a victory roll right over the camp at about one thousand feet!

Or perhaps not a victory roll. The shithouse rumour brigade would be demanding the weapons from their guards, insisting it was all over and we had won!

All in all the officer's visits did me a power of good. At least I knew the men in the camps were not forgotten, and never had been.

My family and Ann's family did a great job with building me up and I put on weight rapidly. The shoulder and hand were still badly wasted, weak and painful, but in a happier environment it was easier to put the pain from my mind for ever longer periods. I concentrated on getting fit and controlling the pain so I could build up the strength in the injured arm. I found it was useless to excercise the arm too much, as the pain became intense. The arm became uncontrollable and almost useless afterwards. So I had to be patient and move things on very slowly.

My leave was for an indefinite period. I was on double rations (ration cards, as per World War II, were still required for some food) and double ration pay. It helped – with my appetite!

I split my time between my home and Ann's home and to help with the travel problem I bought a second-hand motorcycle. A 350cc BSA for £85. The only problem was the clutch control which, being on the left handlebar was meant to be pulled towards the handlebar by the fingers of the left hand being closed. I could not work the clutch in the normal way, but

I managed to use the clutch by curling my fingers around the handle and pulling back with the whole arm. Once I got used to the clutch it was good exercise for the arm. After a few months I had built enough strength into the hand and fingers to use the clutch properly.

The people of Guiting Power, the nearest village to my home, and people from surrounding countryside had a collection for me and raised £50, quite a lot of cash in those days, which they presented to me at a little ceremony in the village hall. I was very grateful for the cash, but very surprised that they should think of doing it. There was no way I could refuse the good folks' gift. But again I was being given something for only doing the job I was paid for. I knew quite well what I was letting myself in for when I joined the Army. The way I saw it, whatever I had to suffer was my own doing, part of the job.

Nevertheless, many years later, in what has become 'another world', I thought back to those good folk of Gloucestershire, their honest, undemonstrative but sincere welcome home (no questions, no hassle, just 'Good to see you home, boy') when I read reports of the treatment meted out to some of the American forces on their return home from Viet Nam.

If the reports are true, that some US Armed Forces were met at airports and docks by hostile, spitting, jeering crowds of fellow Americans, then there is something drastically wrong. It takes all sorts to make a world, and people will voice their opinions but there must have been something lacking in the make-up of the authorities who would allow their men to be subjected to such provocation.

Those men were wearing the uniform of their country. Many of them had thrown their lives on the line and were likely surprised to have survived. Theirs not to reason why, they had done their job as I had done mine many years before. They too deserved, at least, the respect of those who had sent them.

As part of my arm strengthening campaign I made myself a bow and some arrows from local materials, as I had done in my younger days. Even when still at school I had made bows, and arrows which would go right through a five gallon oil drum at about fifteen paces. At first I had to use a very light bow, but as the arm gained strength the bows became stronger and eventually I could send the arrows nearly two hundred yards.

The countryside and woods are the best gymnasium in the world if, like me, you are not put off by rain, wet ground and mud. Running a lot at first caused considerable pain, but as the arm grew stronger so the pain diminished until it was no more painful to run than to stand still.

Apart from regular exercises, I used the arm for anything and everything I could, such as opening doors, playing darts, etc. One thing I could never master was lifting a cup to drink. The arm would tremble too much to control when in the 'drinking position'.

After I had been home for a couple of months I returned to Tidworth Military Hospital for an operation to remove possible residue left behind by the tracer bullet burning in my ribs. There was a lump in my side, quite painful if pressed. They kept me in hospital about three days, during which I had a bogged-up operation with local anaesthetic. Nothing was removed. The anaesthetic wore off at one point and had to be boosted. The so-called surgeon went too deep for the anaesthetic a couple of times and knocked half the clamps off the blood vessels at least once. By the time he gave up he wasn't the only one who had had enough. They decided I would have to return at a later date to have the elusive junk removed under a general anaesthetic. I never did get it removed. There was no way they would have got me back there to be 'put out'.

I thanked my lucky stars the Chinese surgeon who removed the bullet was not like that clown. My complete faith in British and especially British Army doctors took a severe knock at Tidworth but, thank goodness, I have seen that bog-up redeemed many times since.

Another experience with the Army medical scene soon after arriving home was also a bit 'off-putting'. Less than a month after arriving home I was ordered to report to the British Military Hospital at Wheatley, near Oxford, for examination by a neuro-surgeon and a nerve specialist, to re-assess the possibility of an operation to relieve the pain in my arm. Arriving at the appointed time, expecting to stay for a few days I was taken to a ward and given a bed. It was late afternoon when I arrived and I didn't take a lot of notice of my surroundings – being familiar with Military Hospitals.

Then I began to notice something was wrong. I had seen a couple of soldiers with rifles just outside the ward as I entered, but thought nothing of it. At first the other patients in the ward seemed the usual crowd one expects in such places but after a while I realised most of them were acting rather strange. For instance, an oldish sergeant-major had approached me soon after I arrived and told me a joke – something about nuns and penguins – which he seemed to find funnier than I did. Five minutes later he was back, telling me the same joke again. It was after about the fourth or fifth time of hearing the same joke from the same man that I began to look at the other occupants of the ward more closely – and realised they were all mental cases.

The significance of what I then realised was an armed guard in the corridor suddenly tied in with other things I hadn't noticed before – like bars on the windows, heavy padlocks on the emergency fire exit doors and absolutely nothing in the place which was heavy but throwable!

I was imprisoned again. A feeling of panic crept into my mind and became stronger as time passed. I wondered if the Army doctors had found something wrong with my mentality and not told me. Was I expected to go mad at any moment? I thought back over the hectic recent weeks, of my release and journey home. Of the happy times during the last few days. I suddenly felt it would be good to hear that whistle blow – to be a prisoner of war was better than a prisoner in a loony bin.

My mind raced but found no answers, no reasons, no calming facts. I approached an orderly and asked to see the Sister. He said, 'She will be in in a minute, you can see her then.' When I asked again later, another orderly said, 'She has gone off duty now, you'll have to wait until tomorrow.'

What it obviously amounted to – nobody was interested. How could they be? Half the bloody ward wanted to see the sister, the doctor, the CO, (the Queen?). The night did not bring a peaceful sleep, but by morning I had resolved to control my feelings, try to act normal, have faith in myself and my sanity.

I don't remember what I did or said but I must have got through to the sister, and when the matron did her rounds about mid-morning she said she would make some enquiries at once. In fact the matron used the phone in the sister's office, then came back and told me to bring my kit and leave the ward.

It had only been one of those little 'administration bog ups' which bedevil even the best run organisations. The fact that I had been booked in as a nerve case caused it. But it was one of the most terrifying times of my life.

The hospital authorities apologised to me for the mistake and sent me back on leave without seeing the specialists. I think I was on my way home within twenty minutes of leaving the ward, thanking my lucky stars for a sister and a matron who were not just pretty faces, but people who believed in doing their job properly.

When I eventually returned to B.M.H. Wheatley for specialists to see me, several weeks later, I was not detained overnight but was very careful to watch where I was being taken within the hospital – likewise on all subsequent visits! The specialists found there was nothing they could do to help the arm, but they seemed to think I was doing very well on my own.

About four months after my return to UK I had to report to Depot, The Gloucestershire Regiment, Robinswood Camp, Gloucester. Having reported in, I was told to take another month's leave. So back home I went for another month of 'rest and recuperation'.

One thing which bothered me somewhat during those months on leave, another reason I didn't like going into towns. Several times I had a very, very strong feeling I was going to wake up in that camp again. The feeling was so strong one day, when I was standing in Cheltenham High Street, I had a stupid urge to jump in the road under a bus which was passing, so the dream would end before I got to like it too much and the awakening became that much worse.

The pain in my arm was part of the problem. I began to reason with myself, if it was real our people would have stopped that pain by now. The many dreams of release I had in the camp had always been accompanied by pain, so I associated the two to prove one another. Too difficult to explain, but I had several stupid moments and they always happened in town. Luckily I found I already liked the dream too much to end it myself. So I resigned myself to wait for the whistle.

CHAPTER TEN

Gloucester

In 1953 Robinswood Camp, later re-named Robinswood Barracks, contained two units, a Royal Signals detachment and the Glosters Depot. It was an ex-wartime camp, consisting of some red brick, single storey headquarters and administration buildings and a lot of wooden huts to house the troggery. The camp was pretty well spread around, as were most wartime camps, with concrete roads linking most of it loosely together.

Depot Glosters was not much in itself, its Training Wing, however, was relatively large and busy. National Service was in full swing and recruits came in batches of 70 or 80 for eight weeks basic training before being sent out to the battalion which, at that time was in Kenya.

The depot was also a demobilisation centre for the battalion and men who had joined the battalion originally but been transferred to other units. Men came for 'demob' sometimes singly, sometimes in batches of up to one hundred and twenty. So Robinswood Camp saw a continual ebb and flow of troops.

Within twenty minutes of arriving at the camp I was in the 'nick'! It was all rather comical, and it was seeing the funny side of it which put me 'inside'.

Walking along a path towards the orderly room a rather high pitched voice yelled, 'Hey, you'! Not being in the habit of answering to 'hey you' I took no notice. The 'hey you's' got higher, louder and rapidly much nearer. Then it changed to 'That soldier! That man! Stand still!!' (nearly at top 'C').

The clatter of fast approaching ammo boots made me stop and turn. He was about five feet two inches tall but, when he reached me, his jumping in the air was almost making us see eye-to-eye. Only in the physical sense though. He was a sergeant or staff sergeant, well pressed and gleaming, with a big red sash to identify him as depot orderly sergeant. (A daily or weekly duty performed by all sergeants in turn.) We were about two feet apart and he was yelling so loud in his rather high-pitched voice that he couldn't get the words out properly. Eventually it got through to me. 'That is not a path!!' Looking back at the rather well trodden track behind me the thought occurred that even by Army criteria this poor demented little thing had flipped off his rocker.

Probably showed my surprise, if not my pity, so he screamed, 'Read Depot Standing Orders – you will not walk on the grass!!' The sense of humour was difficult to contain and likely showed a bit. I didn't get the next few screeches – too much volume – but then it came through loud and clear – pointing at the guardroom: 'Put yourself inside!!! At the double!! Put yourself inside!!'

Trotting to the guardroom, about a hundred yards away, I collapsed in laughter at the desk and couldn't even speak to the astonished Provost corporal. Five minutes later, having put the Provost staff in the picture the clatter of fast approaching boots of authority were heard and the diminutive DOS appeared in the doorway, a completely changed man, partly because he was now out of sight of the adjutant's office windows. (The adjutant at that time had a hate on 'grass walkers'.)

Within a very short time we had established a common friend – the little sergeant's big brother was on his way home from a Korean POW camp. No charges were made and we were quite good friends from then on. Nevertheless I could still wind him up by saying, 'Mind that grass!'.

My first job at the depot was with the Regimental Police. Being still a private soldier as well as partly crippled there wasn't a lot I could do. At least it got me back into the swing of things while I continued to strengthen my arm and put on weight, but it was not my idea of being useful and was one of the last jobs I would pick, given the choice.

We wore battledress, as did everyone else at that time, but with the rather obvious distinction of white belt and anklets. It brought back memories of my earlier days, in the Corps of Drums, although the 'bull' was not taken to quite such ridiculous extremes and we were not plagued by such stupidities as cheese cutters, (peaked caps) etc.

We were not so much policemen as gate and child minders. Our duties were mostly to do with keeping watch on the main entrance to the camp, checking on who and what came in or out and supervising the lives of men serving short sentences in the guardroom cells. If memory serves me right, there was a Provost corporal and another private soldier like me. The three of us looked after the guardroom, its contents and denizens from 6 a.m. to 6 p.m. The unit provided a six man guard from 6 p.m. to 6 a.m. and at week-ends. It always amused me, when taking over in the morning, to have to sign for 'x' number of live bodies, as well as the guardroom and all its contents, clean and in good order.

While on the Regimental Police only two problems came my way, the rest of it was just a mundane, boring round of bullshit. The first problem was with a deserter we had brought in. He had the reputation of being a very hard man, and had been in the battalion boxing team, a light heavyweight, or something such.

I can't remember what happened, but he wanted out and I happened to be between him and the door. He came at me like a bull at a gate and the first punch didn't put him down, so had to keep hitting because if he found I'd only one arm there would be no hope. Someone told me afterwards, he didn't go down because the wall stopped him.

There were a lot of questions to be answered, but it eventually blew over. The worst bit was taking him to Gloucester Royal Infirmary for X-rays. A very nice sister asked whatever had happened to him. She didn't believe the age-old excuse that he had 'walked into a door'. Especially when he looked hard at me and said, 'Yes, that bloody door!'

If looks could have killed she'd have dropped me on the spot. I couldn't get out of there fast enough – and hoped never to go into the infirmary for anything. Especially X-rays!

The second problem finished me with the Regimental Police. To say my attitude towards the prisoners in the guardroom was too cushy would probably be an understatement. There was a thick early morning fog and it was still quite dark at six o'clock when the prisoners were marched to the cookhouse for their breakfast. Knowing who was duty officer, and knowing there was no way he would be there that early in the morning it was safe enough to give the prisoners a bit of relaxation with American marching patter which, by then, they all knew pretty well. There were about a dozen prisoners, all shouting their parts at full blast: 'You had a good job and you left.' 'You're right,' 'Sound off –' etc. Then the bristling shape of the adjutant loomed out of the fog. He was standing in for the real duty officer. The good old laid back sense of humour as remembered so well from the battalion was totally absent in the depot. I'd had enough of that guardroom anyway!

My next job was chief sweeper, duster, polisher and fire stoker in the education centre. The centre was run by a captain and two sergeants in the Royal Army Education Corps. They were all my type of people, got on with the job, but kept their sense of humour.

After a week or so, the boss man, Captain Bruce Smith, said it would be a good time for me to get my Army 3rd Class Education Certificate. When told I already had it, and my 2nd Class, he wanted to know what the hell I was doing wasting my time at that job. So I told him, and said it might be a good time to get my Army 1st Class. He agreed.

About then, the Army decided it would have Unit Education Instructors. A course was being assembled within a week or two, and before I knew it Bruce Smith had me on the list and off to 16 Army Education Centre at Bovington, Dorset.

There were two Other Ranks on the course, the other being a lance corporal from REME. The rest were all officers, warrant officers and sergeants. About twenty of us altogether. I passed the course quite well, coming top with a 45 minute test lecture and fairly well up with the rest of it.

Returning to Gloucester, I got stuck into a more interesting job. It came as a bit of a shock to teach classes of National Servicemen to read and write. (And I mean from scratch, like – cat, mat, bat, etc.) I found I had a knack for getting men to ask me to write letters home for them – then read the answers next week! They took their inability to read and write as something the Army was going to put right for them and that attitude of mind made for easy teaching. All were keen to learn. We all enjoyed the classes which came as a welcome relief from the drill square, etc. A couple or three months went by and I was sent on an NCO's course at the Devons' Depot, which was also the Wessex Brigade Depot, at Exeter.

Coming back after six weeks of mostly bullshit, with a brand new tape on my arm, I found I had lost my job. The Army had decided I hadn't the qualifications to go on the Education Instructors Course, (already passed) therefore must be taken off the Instruction job. Bruce Smith sent off a lot of letters, made a lot of 'phone calls, to no avail.

Just before being sent on the NCO course I had started studying for my Army Certificate of Education 1st Class. The course disrupted my study programme, and the exam was the week after returning. I got three subjects out of the required five so it wasn't wasted, and could take the other two when the next exams came round – if I had time.

My next job at Depot Glosters was in the Quartermaster's Stores. The QM was Jack Hobbs, who had been RSM 1st Glosters in Korea. He had been captured the day after me but had done two and a quarter years in the camp as he wasn't released until the war finished.

The Armistice, to end military conflict in the Korean War, had been signed on 27 July 1953; the ex-POW's came home in September and October after a long boat trip. Soon after, we had a great re-union in Gloucester, and a remembrance parade followed by a service in Gloucester Cathedral.

Jack Hobbs was a great character, who had a good sense of humour. He got on well with his staff in the QM Department. I enjoyed my time there. I can't remember the date when I went to the QM Stores, it must have been April or May 1954, and I worked there until about March 1957. In that time my arm made a good recovery. It wasn't perfect by a long way, but it was usable.

In 1955 Ann and I were married. We set up home in a flat over an old farmhouse at Longford, just north of Gloucester. Those were happy days, we spent many weekends at our parents' homes and seemed to be on the go somewhere or other all the time.

One Friday evening in summer we decided to tour Devon and Cornwall. I had bought a bigger bike – a BSA 500cc twin, which went well. We threw a case on the back, put three army blankets and two ponchos in my Army kit bag (sleeping bags were not common in those days) and hit the road. Just after dark we found a good spot on Exmoor and slept under the stars. The next night we were under the stars somewhere near Land's End. On the Sunday the weather changed about mid-afternoon, so we went back to Gloucester for Sunday night.

Easy enough now with the motorways and straightened roads, but in those days it was hard riding and we could hardly get off the bike when we arrived home. Nevertheless, we must have been through at least three quarters of the 'sea-side' towns in Devon and Cornwall – and really enjoyed ourselves.

Usually, when I had to work late in the stores due to an extra large intake of National Servicemen, Jack Hobbs would appear, rip off his jacket and get stuck in to help with preparing the kit for issue. On a few occasions, when she claimed she had nothing better to do, Ann would come and give me a hand.

The main problem with 'other people' in a QM Store is making sure they don't 'liberate' anything while your back is turned. With Ann it was the opposite. I once caught her slipping the odd bar of chocolate into kit bags we were preparing. Claimed she couldn't bear to think of all those 'poor little lads being dragged away from their mothers'. My comments about what it might cost us in chocolate to make up for about a hundred doting mums went unheeded, – as usual! But I made sure she bought no more goodies to bolster the morale of the Army. Every six months I had to go up to Wheatley, near Oxford, to see a specialist who checked my arm was making satisfactory progress. He was very pleased with the way things were going, which is more than could be said for myself. Thought I would crack it in six months. It took four years! For that four years my medical grade was P.7 – the lowest grade allowed before compulsory discharge from the Army. Try as I might there just was no quick way. Patience was not my strongest virtue either, but there was nothing for it except exercise and wait. Time would do the most.

When I saw the specialist in September 1956, he said if it kept improving he would upgrade me to P.3 (or something) the next time he saw me. Told him P.3 was no good to me, if I wasn't graded fully fit I might as well stay at P.7.

Working in the QM Stores it was my job to take the Army kit from men being demobbed, and during the last few months two SAS men had come for demob. One of them had helped me in the stores for a week or two, waiting for his discharge date. I found out as much as possible about the SAS as until these SAS men appeared I had understood the unit had been disbanded after World War II. Finding the unit had been reformed for the jungle war in Malaya, I knew where I had to go. The only problem was the arm.

On telling the specialist at Wheatley why I wanted to be

graded fit, he laughed in my face. He said I'd never make it – 'They have to parachute and God knows what else!' Nevertheless, he agreed that if I could improve enough to be up-graded – it would be 'F.E.' or nothing.

A lot of hard work went into the next six months. Not only to strengthen the arm, but also to strengthen the power of mind over matter to shut out the pain. The pain is always there if I think about it, the trick is never to think about it. When it screams – ignore it. Ann had to put up with some stick when I had nightmares of agony. A happy marriage helps as much as anything with problems like mine, so I was getting all the help possible. At one stage Ann had threatened to report me to the MO if I didn't go and get something for the pain. There were times when I had to take pain-killers, but it felt like an admission of failure. All the time my medical grade was P.7 I was excused about everything except breathing. No drill, no parades, no guard duties (even excused wearing braces to keep up my trousers!) I only had to see the MO to get a few days off.

I did my work, always starting before those who had to appear on the morning parade, and very often working late at night to get finished when we had a new intake of recruits, or a big demobbing session. I never once asked for time off.

I made damn sure I never did any parades, drill or guard duties. It was often said in the Glosters, if the men of years ago had known the problems they would inflict upon future generations of the regiment by standing back to back, they would have thrown their hand in.

The men I have seen in trouble over their back badge must number dozens. It had to be highly polished both sides, also the split pin which held it in place. It was quite usual for several men on any parade to have to take their badges from their berets so the reverse side could be inspected.

The thing which got me most about this practice was the officer who was keenest on it. He always had the top button of his battledress blouse undone. He also always came on parade with his battledress cuffs turned up. Then had the damned hard neck to charge and punish any soldier he could find with a speck of 'brasso' on the back of his back badge.

March 1957 came at last, and off I went to Wheatley. The specialist was surprised at the improvement. He asked if I still intended to join the SAS. I told him the application was already made out. He wished me the best of luck and upgraded me, completely fit. The next morning my application for transfer to SAS went into Depot Headquarters – before my upgrading had arrived from Wheatley.

Arriving at the QM Department, I went to see Jack. He saw my determination to go through with it and wished me luck. He also said he would be leaving soon, to go as QM to the battalion, and had wanted me to go with him as 'Tech' Sergeant. (By that time I had two tapes, so it would have been a natural enough move.) I thanked Jack for his confidence in me, but said my mind was definitely made up.

Later that day, the shit hit the fan! The RSM sent for me and said the adjutant wanted to know what was this crap about the SAS. I told him about the up-grading to FE the day before. It was a genuine application for transfer. He went off, presumably to see the adjutant, and came back five minutes later with a lot of waffle about the Glosters had 'carried' me for four years when I was 'supposedly' too sick to do my duty properly, etc. etc. etc.

When he had finished he stared at me hard, then said 'Well, what have you got to say for yourself?' The old temper was beginning to rise so, as quietly as I could I said, 'I have been medically up-graded, sir, and have applied for transfer to the Special Air Service Regiment.' The RSM stared hard for a long time then yelled 'Get out!' about four times. I was outside the office before he had finished. He had done his duty – for the benefit of other ears. I didn't blame him. In fact, before I left Depot Glosters he shook hands and wished me luck.

A week or so later I handed over the QM Stores and was sent to Training Wing. There was method in their madness. In Training Wing I took over the Continuation Training Platoon. The platoon was made up entirely of young regular soldiers, about 40 of them, who had joined the Army at seventeen and a half years old, done their eight weeks' basic training, but were not old enough to be sent to the battalion (as it was in an operational area) until they were eighteen.

They were young, thought they were rough and tough and, more to the point, had busted every NCO who had ever had the misfortune to be put in charge of them. It didn't take long to see the problem. I looked at the names of those 'busted' and realised that, with only one exception, they were inexperienced

NCO's who had never even been to the battalion. One or two had even been National Servicemen. I knew, from my own not so distant youth, what this lot wanted and needed: hard nasty training and less bullshit, less drill square.

All they seemed to have done was drill, until they were sick of it. I knew the feeling well! Looking through the platoon's old training programmes was easy. There it was – drill, inserted over weapon training, over field training, and so on.

So instead of parading at 7.45 a.m. for the usual drill, I had them parade at 7.30 a.m. in battle order. By 7.45 a.m. we had drawn weapons and haversack rations and were going out of camp at the double, with me giving them a dog's life. Once clear of the built-up area, we were into ack-ack formation, making a good pace.

I can't remember how many miles we did that first day. We had our mid-day stop on Painswick Beacon and arrived back at camp about 4.00 p.m. By which time a lot of them were not feeling or looking so tough. I had the stronger, fitter men carry the rifles and packs of the weaker ones. We went back through the camp gate at the double, in rough formation.

The training got rougher and tougher, but so did the men. They enjoyed every minute of it. This was what they had joined the Army for.

A couple of times we had to help with night demonstrations. One night in particular I remember well. The demonstration was for a company of Army Cadets. Part of it entailed me leading a section along a path in the darkness to demonstrate different actions to be taken when illuminated by various things such as trip flares, Very lights, headlamps, etc. One of the 'etceteras' was supposed to be a smoke grenade which would silhouette us. The plan was for me to drop the smoke grenade by the side of the track as I walked along, with the section following.

I was given the grenade by an officer, and even in the dark I realised he had given me an 80 grenade, which is a phosphorous grenade and can be a killer. I pointed out the mistake and told him I would not use it as instructed. He told me it was harmless, and gave me a direct order to use the grenade as instructed. Tried to argue, but it was no use. I had used 80 grenades in Korea, and seen their effects at close range, so there was no way I was going to be anywhere handy when that thing went off!!!

Everything went as planned until it came to the 'smoke'

grenade when, orders or no orders, I heaved it as far as I could. White phosphorous is quite spectacular at night and I enjoyed the thoughts of what certain officers were thinking when it exploded. It was the end of the demonstration and a couple of people came rushing to us asking if anyone was hurt. Altogether it was quite an enjoyable evening. I did spare a thought, however, for the consequences had I been another National Service Junior NCO – or even, God forbid, an officer!

We had no problems for a few weeks, then one Friday afternoon, someone up there insisted we appear on Saturday morning RSM's Drill Parade. The platoon could do most anything with a rifle now – except drill.

I had them parade outside their huts at 6.00 p.m. Friday night and tried to knock them into their old shape again. They tried hard, but I knew we were for it in the morning.

The form of the Drill Parade came to my aid. Platoons were drilled separately by their NCO's and the RSM went from one to another, attacking each platoon separately. I picked the right patch of drill square, gave the platoon arms drill 'at the halt' until the RSM was nearly to us. Then I went mad over their sloppiness, had them hold their rifles over their heads and doubled them off around the edge of the square, all the time giving them a dog's life. The platoon suffered but the RSM never caught up with us. After that we had to do the odd bit of drill to keep out of trouble on Saturdays.

While on that job at Training Wing, I was sometimes required to go and help on the grenade range, with the National Servicemen. This was an eye-opener to me. Never did I think men could be so nervous, or that nerves could affect men so much. They could be trained to near perfection with dummy grenades, but there were always the odd two or three in a platoon who went all to pieces when it came to the real thing. Either they would let go too soon, so the grenade would go straight up in the air and come back down in the trench, or they would hang on too long, hit the bank in front of the trench so the grenade rolled back in. It was then my job to get them out of the trench before the grenade exploded. Those grenades exploded four seconds after the man let go, so time wasn't going spare.

One of the things which made me determined to pass SAS Selection was the attitude of one of the depot officers. After I applied for transfer he would not salute me when he met me around camp. When I saluted he looked the other way. This tickled me pink and it's a good job he never looked, or he would have caught the big stupid grin on my face.

I was saluting the Queen's uniform so it didn't bother me that the clown wearing it acted like a big kid! The final touch came when my transfer finally came through. It is normal practice in the Army for men leaving a unit to appear before their CO for a pep talk or whatever, before they go. But in my case it so happened that I had to be interviewed by the officer who refused to salute me, or even recognise my presence.

The time came, I was ordered to Headquarters for the interview, quite interested to see how it would be handled – eyeball to eyeball. He didn't have the guts. The interview was carried out – wait for it – on the telephone, through the adjutant, in the adjutant's office! I wasn't even allowed to soil the office carpet. Standing there, hardly believing it, I wondered how that gentleman would look under Section 42 of the Army Act – 'Conduct to the prejudice of good order and military discipline' – if I burst out laughing! By contrast, the good old Continuation Training Platoon made sure they didn't bust me, and gave me five hundred cigarettes and a lighter when I left.

So ended my 'Infantry experience'. Again I was leaving many good friends behind. Apart from the odd clown, the Glosters were – and most likely still are – a damn good unit.

I would like to think the air of laid back, confident efficiency which, to me, was the outstanding characteristic of the Gloucestershire Regiment in the Imjin battle, had somehow been carried on through the years to the present day.

As a young, inexperienced soldier I was no doubt influenced by the attitude of those older, well experienced men around me. Their unflappable example made me better able to cope, to do my bit, as did hundreds of other trogs in 29 Brigade. Most of us were able to do our job to the best of our ability, but there were those who responded beyond the call of duty and performed feats of courage and endurance under the most horrific conditions. Many of these are known only to a few amazed onlookers, but some were rewarded by receiving a medal for their bravery. It is well known, in most circles, that the British Army does not treat medals confetti-wise! but the

Honours and Awards list for the Glosters who took part in the Imjin battle gives some indication as to the number of men whose bravery was above the norm.

1st Battalion, Gloucestershire Regiment during the Imjin River Battle, 22-25 April 1951, earned two Victoria Crosses, two DSOs, one MBE, three MC's, two DCM's, eight MM's, three BEM's and forty two officers and men were Mentioned in Despatches. 1st Glosters, and 'C' Troop, 170th Independent Mortar Battery, Royal Artillery were each awarded the United States Presidential Distinguished Unit Citation.

The spirits of units like the Glosters can surely never die while they remain active units within the Army. They will have their ups and downs – and, no doubt, their clown problems – but, in the end, come the crunch, the same spirit would again sustain men in the face of overwhelming odds, should the need arise. Over the many years now, since the Korean war, people have often asked me if I think of Korea or remember anything about it.

As far as remembering goes, this book must speak for itself. I kept no diaries or records of any kind during my military service. The dates quoted are correct from reference to various documents and factual histories such as *The Imjin Roll* by Colonel E.D. Harding DSO (my highly regarded company commander during the Imjin battle), but more often from reference to my Record of Army Service. The days and dates, Sunday 22 April to Wednesday 25 April 1951 are stamped into my memory forever.

Do I ever think of Korea or the Korean war? Yes, I think of the Korean war, just as thousands of others who have been left with constant reminders. However, I count myself extremely fortunate not only to have survived the experience but to have lived my life more or less as I've wished ever since.

The memories, even so, are there if one digs deep enough. In the course of my writing I have, on occasion, dug too deep. The sight, the sound, the smell, the feel have all come back. Not good news.

Korea, Land of the Morning Calm was, to me, not all war, destruction and despair. It can be a very beautiful country, especially in the autumn, when the hills and mountains with their cloak of trees display all the vivid colours of nature.

Perhaps my view of Korea in the autumn, which was of

course from the confines of a prison camp, was also coloured by the fact that what I could see was outside the camp, therefore representing freedom, the outside world, untouched by the squalor, death and disease of my immediate surroundings.

Nevertheless, it is a beautiful country.

Glossary

BAOR	– British Army of the Rhine (Area of Germany occupied by British Forces).
BMH	– British Military Hospital
Blitzkrieg	– Lightning War (German)
Blighty	– UK
Bullshit	– That which supposedly baffles brains –
	(a) By Actions, such as polishing, painting, scrubbing, pressing and 'smartening' to a point far in excess of clean and tidy.
	(b) By Talking, a load of crap.
Chopper	– Helicopter
CQB	– Close quarter battle.
Demob	– Demobilisation. (Discharge from the Armed Forces).
ETA	– Estimated Time of Arrival.
FGA	– Fighter Ground Attack (Aircraft)
Last light	– Dusk. Sundown.
NAAFI	– Navy, Army & Air Force Institute (British Forces Canteen).
OP	– Observation Point or Observation Position.
POW	– Prisoner of War.
PT	– Physical Training.
Recce	– Reconnaissance.
RNF	– Royal Northumberland Fusiliers.
RSM	– Regimental Sergeant Major.
RUR	– Royal Ulster Rifles.
RV	– Rendezvous. Meeting Place.
Sangar	– Rock wall, often in a circle, where firing positions cannot be dug into ground.
SAS	– Special Air Service.

Weapons

LMG	– Light Machine Gun.

SMG	— Sub Machine Gun.
Sten	— British Sub Machine Gun 9mm 32 round box magazine
.30 Cal:	— (Point) thirty (inch) calibre Browning (US) medium machine gun.
.50 Cal:	— (Point) fifty (inch) calibre Browning (US) heavy machine gun. Also called 'Point Five'.
36 Grenade	— British High Explosive Shrapnel Grenade.
80 Grenade	— British White Phosphorous Grenade.
Stick Grenade	— Possibly a Chinese version of the old Japanese 'stick grenade' used up to and during World War II.
Burp Gun	(a) Russian PPSh 1941G. Most seen in action were loaded with 71 round Drum magazine. Very few had box magazines.
	(b) Chinese version known as Type 50. All seen were using 35 round Box magazine.
	— Both models were 7.62mm and had a rate of fire of approx: 900 rounds per minute.
Rifle	(a) British — No.4 Enfield. Bolt action. .303 inch
	(b) Chinese — Simenov (Soviet) semi-automatic. 7.62mm with folding bayonet. Most common in forward units. In rear areas there were many types of old bolt action rifles, practically no semi-automatic rifles.
Bren, Light Machine Gun	(a) British. — .303 30 round magazine
	(b) Chinese. Most were Chinese made .30 cal: with 20 round magazines.
Tommy Gun	— American Thompson Sub Machine Gun .45 Cal. About half with 50 round drum magazine, half with 20 round box magazine.

Index

General

Aden, 27
Aldershot, 11
Americans, 36, 39, 84, 97, 101, 102, 106, 113, 115, 131, 132, 136, 141, 143, 145, 152, 159
  Aircrew officers, 122
  Artillery, 42
  Coloured, 128
  Forces, 38
  Germ warfare, 123
  Infantry, 54
  Jet fighters, 122
  Military Police, 37, 39, 40
  Officers POW, 95
  Pilot, 89
  POWs, 88, 89, 93, 95, 96, 97, 98, 124, 139
  POW deaths, 96
  POW shot, 91
  Tanks, 96
  Troops, 38, 114
  Trucks, 85
  Units, *see* 'US Armed Forces'
Ann, 25, 31, 104, 105, 149, 150, 151, 161, 162, 163
Anzio, 43
Arab, 26
Arnhem, 28
Australian, 35, 78, 104, 135
Austria, 100

Baker (Wilts Regt), 22
Baker, Corp George, 67, 68, 69, 79, 80, 86
Barrington, Ken, 29
Belgians, 42
Beri-Beri, 102, 103, 104
Birmingham, 116
'Black Treacle Warfare', 124
'Boot Hill', 96, 139
Bovington, 160
British, 9, 10, 37, 39, 77, 79, 85, 91, 95, 113, 124, 128, 131, 142, 143, 153
  Armed Forces Special Voucher (Baffs), 88

BBC Overseas Service, 132
Communists, 136, 137
Communist Party, 118, 119, 136
Infantry, 27
Infantry weapons and equipment, 46
Officers, 143, 144
Red Cross, 143, 144, 145
POWs, 73, 93, 94, 96, 97, 101, 106, 114, 133, 134, 136, 141, 144, 150
POW 'cooks', 129
Traitor, 135
Troops, 78, 136
Units, *see* 'British and Commonwealth Forces'
Brodie, Brig, 43
BSA, 151, 161
Buckingham Palace, 27
Budapest, 105
Burma, 43

Canadians, 78
Carne, Lt-Col J.P., 40, 50, 81, 126, 127
Castlepeak Bay, 32
Ceylon, 148
'Char Wallah', 30, 31
Cheltenham, 12, 120, 121, 127, 132, 149, 155
'Chelt Nam Peoples Army', 132
China, 38, 59, 101, 113, 114, 147
Chinese, 50, 55, 62, 67, 73, 78, 79, 81, 82, 84, 89, 90, 96-102, 105, 106, 109, 115, 116, 119-24, 127-9, 131, 132, 134-6, 141, 142, 145, 147
Border, 84
Camouflage, 72, 85
Casualties, 54, 65, 66, 77, 86, 147
Character, 33
Doctor, 139, 140
Firepower, 46
Forces, 114
Garrison, 93
Guard, 120, 124, 128, 130
Infantry, 42, 59